AF199090

# Driving Performance at Peru's Water and Sanitation Services Regulator

OECD

BETTER POLICIES FOR BETTER LIVES

This document, as well as any data and map included herein, are without prejudice to the status of or sovereignty over any territory, to the delimitation of international frontiers and boundaries and to the name of any territory, city or area.

The statistical data for Israel are supplied by and under the responsibility of the relevant Israeli authorities. The use of such data by the OECD is without prejudice to the status of the Golan Heights, East Jerusalem and Israeli settlements in the West Bank under the terms of international law.

Note by Turkey
The information in this document with reference to "Cyprus" relates to the southern part of the Island. There is no single authority representing both Turkish and Greek Cypriot people on the Island. Turkey recognises the Turkish Republic of Northern Cyprus (TRNC). Until a lasting and equitable solution is found within the context of the United Nations, Turkey shall preserve its position concerning the "Cyprus issue".

Note by all the European Union Member States of the OECD and the European Union
The Republic of Cyprus is recognised by all members of the United Nations with the exception of Turkey. The information in this document relates to the area under the effective control of the Government of the Republic of Cyprus.

**Please cite this publication as:**
OECD (2022), *Driving Performance at Peru's Water and Sanitation Services Regulator*, The Governance of Regulators, OECD Publishing, Paris, *https://doi.org/10.1787/89f3ccee-en*.


ISBN 978-92-64-50871-2 (print)
ISBN 978-92-64-95199-0 (pdf)


The Governance of Regulators
ISSN 2415-1432 (print)
ISSN 2415-1440 (online)

# Foreword

Economic regulators play an important role in ensuring the affordability, quality and accessibility of essential services, such as water and sanitation. The stakes are high: regulators' actions affect outcomes for consumers and can have major social and environmental implications. Exogenous shocks, such as the COVID-19 pandemic, make balancing these outcomes even more challenging. Economic regulators are expected to provide stability for markets and investors, and to design regulations that protect the public interest without impeding innovation. Good governance is essential to ensure the effectiveness of the regulator and support better outcomes, especially in times of change.

Over the past decade, Peru has placed water security high on its political agenda, but wider governance challenges have jeopardised policy continuity and delivery. Recent political and social turmoil have had an impact on the effective implementation of public policies, including water and sanitation. This report applies the OECD Performance Assessment Framework for Economic Regulators (PAFER) to Peru's economic regulator for water and sanitation services (*Superintendencia Nacional de Servicios de Saneamiento*, Sunass), upon invitation of the regulator.

The PAFER review finds that Sunass is a technically sound and ambitious regulator that is making strides to improve regulatory practices and deliver on an expanded mandate. The regulator operates in a challenging context that complicates the urgent task of increasing access to safe drinking water and sanitation services. The review recommends that Sunass communicate proactively on risks and expectations, and expand its regulatory toolkit to promote behavioural change. To do so, Sunass needs to consolidate its institutional transformation, update its identity and culture, and strengthen external collaboration and co-ordination across its regional offices as well as with key actors in the sector.

The OECD has developed the PAFER framework to support regulators in assessing and strengthening their organisational performance and governance structures. The framework, based on the *OECD Best Practice Principles on the Governance of Regulators*, analyses regulators' internal and external governance, including their organisational structures, behaviour, accountability, processes, reporting and performance management, as well as role clarity, relationships, distribution of powers and responsibilities with other government and non-government stakeholders.

This report builds on existing OECD work on the water sector in Peru, notably the two-year Water Governance Policy Dialogue in Peru led by the OECD Centre for Entrepreneurship, SMEs, Regions and Cities (CFE) that culminated in the publication *Water Governance in Peru* in March 2021.

This report is part of the OECD work programme on the governance of regulators and regulatory policy, led by the OECD Network of Economic Regulators and the OECD Regulatory Policy Committee, with the support of the Regulatory Policy Division of the OECD Directorate of Public Governance. The Directorate's mission is to help government at all levels design and implement strategic, evidence-based and innovative policies that support sustainable economic and social development. The report was presented to the OECD Network of Economic Regulators for comments and approval at its 17th meeting in November 2021 and declassified by written procedure by the Regulatory Policy Committee on 4 January 2022. It was prepared for publication by the Secretariat.

# Acknowledgements

This report was prepared by the OECD Public Governance Directorate (GOV), under the leadership and with the encouragement and support of Elsa Pilichowski, Director; János Bertók, Deputy Director; and Nick Malyshev, Head of the Regulatory Policy Division, GOV. It was co-ordinated and drafted by Martha Baxter and Vincent van Langen with significant inputs from Alberto Morales and Roberto Arana Fierros, under the guidance and supervision of Anna Pietikainen. Ana Simion carried out initial preparatory work. Substantive comments were provided by Nick Malyshev, Florentin Blanc and Alberto Morales of GOV.

Jennifer Stein co-ordinated the editorial process and Andrea Uhrhammer provided editorial support. Johanna Palmi provided administrative support. The translation of the report into Spanish was prepared by Gilda Moreno Manzur.

The team included three peer reviewers, who participated in a virtual policy mission to Peru and provided extensive inputs and feedback throughout the development of the review: Andrea Guerrini, Commissioner of ARERA, the Italian Regulatory Authority for Energy, Networks and Environment; Sanford Berg, Professor Emeritus, Economics, at the University of Florida; and Maria Cristina Portugal, President, Portugal's Energy Services Regulatory Authority, ERSE. The team would like to pay special tribute to Maria Cristina Portugal who passed away in September 2021, and thank her colleagues at ERSE, especially Mariana Pereira, Member of the Board, Natalie McCoy, Head of International Affairs, and Ana Filipa Santos, International Affairs, for their support to preparing and continuing ERSE's engagement with the review.

The report would not have been possible without the support of Sunass and its staff. The team would like to thank in particular the following colleagues for their valuable assistance in collecting data and information, for their support and flexibility to organising and conducting the team's missions remotely, as well as for providing feedback at different stages of the review: Iván Lucich Larrauri, Executive President; Ana María Fox Joo, Lucy Henderson Palacios, Lucía Delfina Ruiz Ostoic, Richard Alberto Navarro Rodríguez, Members of the Board of Directors; José Manuel Zavala Muñoz, General Manager; and Roger Loyola Gonzales, Advisor in the General Management. The team would also like to thank all those that participated in the interviews during the review process, including the various Sunass departments, government, industry and civil society stakeholders, which contributed to the analysis presented in the report.

# Table of contents

**FIGURES**

## TABLES

# Abbreviations and acronyms

| | |
|---|---|
| **ADERASA** | Association of Water and Sanitation Regulatory Bodies of the Americas (*Asociación de Entes Reguladores de Agua y Saneamiento de las Americas*) |
| **AIRHSP** | Software Application for the Centralized Record of Payrolls and Human Resources Data of the Public Sector (*Aplicativo Informático para el Registro Centralizado de Planillas y de Datos de los Recursos Humanos*) |
| **ANA** | National Water Authority (*Autoridad Nacional de Agua*) |
| **APCI** | Agency for International Cooperation (*Agencia Peruana de Cooperación Internacional*) |
| **ATM** | Municipal Technical Areas (*Áreas Técnicas Municipales*) |
| **CAP** | Staff Assignment Chart (*Cuadro para Asignación de Personal*) |
| **CAP-P** | Cadre for Assignment of Provisional Staff (*Cuadro para Asignación de Personal Provisional*) |
| **CAS** | Administrative contracting of services (*Contratación Administrativa de Servicios*) |
| **CEPLAN** | National Center for Strategic Planning (*Centro Nacional de Planeamiento Estratégico*) |
| **CGR** | Comptroller General of the Republic (*Contraloría General de la República del Perú*) |
| **CU** | Users Councils (*Consejo de Usuarios*) |
| **DAP** | Service Area Directorate (*Dirección de Ámbito de la Prestación*) |
| **DATASS** | Rural Water, Sanitation and Hygiene Information System (*Sistema de Diagnóstico sobre Abastecimiento de Agua y Saneamiento en el Ámbito Rural*) |
| **DF** | Supervision Directorate (*Dirección de Fiscalización*) |
| **DGAA** | General Office of Environmental Affairs (*Dirección General de Asuntos Ambientales*) |
| **DIGESA** | General Office of Environmental Health (*Dirección General de Salud Ambiental*) |
| **DPN** | Policy and Regulations Directorate (*Dirección de Políticas y Normas*) |
| **DRT** | Tariff Regulation Directorate (*Dirección de Regulación Tarifaria*) |
| **DS** | Sanctions Directorate (*Dirección de Sanciones*) |
| **DU** | Users Directorate (*Dirección de Usuarios*) |
| **ENAPRES** | National Survey of Budget Programs (*Encuesta Nacional de Programas Presupuestales*) |
| **EPs** | Sanitation Service Providers (*Empresas Prestadoras del Servicio de Saneamiento*) |
| **GRD** | Disaster Risk Management (*Gestión del Riesgo de Desastres*) |

| | |
|---|---|
| **IGPSS** | Index of the Management of Sanitation Services Provision (*Índice de Gestión de la Prestación de los Servicios de Saneamiento*) |
| **INACAL** | National Quality Institute (*Instituto Nacional de Calidad*) |
| **INAIGEM** | National Research Institute of Glacier and Mountain Ecosystems (*Instituto Nacional de Investigación en Glaciares y Ecosistemas de Montaña*) |
| **INDECOPI** | National Institute for the Defence of Competition and the Protection of Intellectual Property (*Instituto Nacional de Defensa de la Competencia y de la Protección de la Propiedad Intelectual*) |
| **INEI** | National Statistics Institute (*Instituto Nacional de Estadística e Informática*) |
| **JASS** | Community-organised water and sanitation services boards (*Junta Administradora de Servicios de Saneamiento*) |
| **MAV** | Maximum Allowable Values |
| **MEF** | Ministry of Economy and Finance (*Ministerio de Economía y Finanzas*) |
| **MERESE** | Mechanisms of Rewards for Ecosystem Services (*Mecanismos de Retribución por servicios Ecosistémicos*) |
| **MINAM** | Ministry of Environment (*Ministerio del Ambiente*) |
| **MINSA** | Ministry of Health (*Ministerio de Salud*) |
| **MOF** | Organisation and Duties Handbook (*Manual de Organización y Funciones*) |
| **MPL** | Maximum Permissible Limits |
| **MTPE** | Ministry of Labour and Employment Promotion (*Ministerio de Trabajo y Promoción del Empleo*) |
| **MVCS** | Ministry of Housing, Construction and Sanitation, (*Ministerio de Vivienda, Construcción y Saneamiento*) |
| **OAF** | Office of Administration and Finance (*Oficina de Administración y Finanzas*) |
| **OAJ** | Office of Legal Advice (*Oficina de Asesoría Jurídica*) |
| **OCI** | Institutional Control Body (*Órgano de Control Institucional*) |
| **OCII** | Office of Communications and Institutional Image (*Oficina de Comunicaciones e Imagen Institucional*) |
| **ODS** | Decentralised offices (*Oficinas Descentralizadas*) |
| **OECD** | Organisation for Economic Co-operation and Development |
| **OEFA** | Environmental Assessment and Control Agency (*Organismo de Evaluación y Fiscalización Ambiental*) |
| **OEI** | Institutional Strategic Objectives (*Objetivos Estratégicos Institucionales*) |
| **OPPM** | Office of Planning, Budget and Modernisation (*Oficina de Planificación, Presupuesto y Modernización*) |
| **OSINERGMIN** | Energy Investment Supervisory Agency (*Organismo Supervisor de la Inversión en Energía y Minería*) |
| **OSIPTEL** | Supervisory Body for Private Investment in Telecommunications (*Organismo Supervisor de Inversión Privada en Telecomunicaciones*) |
| **OTASS** | Technical Organization for the Administration of Sanitation Services (*Organismo Técnico de la Administración de los Servicios de Saneamiento*) |
| **OTI** | Office of IT (*Oficina de Tecnologías de Información*) |

| | |
|---|---|
| **PAFER** | Performance Assessment Framework for Economic Regulators |
| **PCC** | Quality Control Plan (*Plan de Control de Calidad del Agua*) |
| **PCM** | Presidency of the Council of Ministers (*Presidencia del Consejo de Ministros*) |
| **PDP** | People Development Plan (*Plan de Desarrollo de las Personas*) |
| **PEI** | Institutional Strategic Plan (*Plan Estratégico Institucional*) |
| **PESEM** | Multiannual Sectoral Strategic Plan (*Plan Estratégico Sectorial Multianual*) |
| **PIA** | Opening Institutional Budget (*Presupuesto Institucional de Apertura*) |
| **PIM** | Modified Institutional Budget (*Presupuesto Institucional Modificado*) |
| **POI** | Multiannual Operational Plan (*Plan Operativo Institucional Multianual*) |
| **PPP** | Public-Private Partnership |
| **PROINVERSION** | Private Investment Promotion Agency (*Agencia de Promoción de la Inversión Privada*) |
| **PSE** | Payment for Ecosystem Services (*Pagos por Servicios Ecosistémicos*) |
| **RAT** | Transitional Support Regime (*Régimen de Apoyo Transitorio*) |
| **RegWAS-LAC** | Improvement of Public Policies and Regulation of Water and Sanitation Services Programme in Latin America and the Caribbean (*Programa de Mejora de las Políticas Públicas y la Regulación de los Servicios de Agua y Saneamiento en América Latina y el Caribe*) |
| **RIA** | Regulatory Impact Analysis |
| **ROF** | Organisational Duties Regulation (*Reglamento de Organización y Funciones*) |
| **RREE** | Ministry of Foreign Affairs (*Ministerio de Relaciones Exteriores*) |
| **SENAMHI** | National Service of Meteorology and Hydrology of Peru (*Servicio Nacional de Meteorología e Hidrología del Perú*) |
| **SERVIR** | National Civil Service Authority (*Autoridad Nacional del Servicio Civil*) |
| **SIAF** | Integrated Administrative Financial System (*Sistemas Integrados de Administración Financiera*) |
| **SIAS** | Water and Sanitation Information System (*Sistema de Información de Agua y Saneamiento*) |
| **SICAP** | Data Capture and Transfer System (*Sistema de Captura y Transferencia de Datos*) |
| **SIIGEPSS** | System of Indicators and Indices for the Management of Sanitation Services Providers (*Sistema de Indicadores e Índices de la Gestión de los Prestadores de los Servicios de Saneamiento*) |
| **SNC** | National Control System (*Sistema Nacional de Control*) |
| **Sunass** | National Superintendency of Sanitation Services (*Superintendencia Nacional de Servicios de Saneamiento*) |
| **TRASS** | Administrative Tribunal for the Settlement of Sanitation Users' Claims (*Tribunal Administrativo de Solución de Reclamos de los Usuarios de los Servicios de Saneamiento*) |
| **TSC** | Dispute Settlement Tribunal (*Tribunal de Solución de Controversias*) |
| **WSS** | Water and Sanitation Services |

# Executive summary

The National Superintendency of Sanitation Services (*Superintendencia Nacional de Servicios de Saneamiento*, Sunass) is Peru's independent economic regulator for drinking water, sewerage treatment and sanitary disposal of excreta. The regulator operates in a challenging national and sectoral context, where only 51% of population has access to safely managed drinking water services.

Since its creation in 1992, Sunass has established itself as a technically sound regulator. In 2016, the regulator was entrusted with an expanded mandate. Originally responsible for regulating the country's 50 urban water utilities, its new scope encompasses over 25 000 providers across the entire national territory. Sunass also became responsible for a number of new tasks, some of which go beyond the core regulatory functions shared by Peruvian sector regulators. In response to these changes, Sunass has undertaken a significant institutional transformation, including the establishment of 24 regional offices.

Going forward, Sunass should engage proactively with stakeholders to manage risks and expectations regarding the implementation of the regulator's expanded mandate, improve role clarity, and identify areas where enhanced collaboration and co-ordination can support the achievement of policy goals. Crucially, a fit-for-purpose regulatory toolbox will be needed to ensure appropriate incentives to drive sector performance and increase the regulator's impact. Furthermore, a consolidated identity and culture can ensure the coherence of approaches across the reformed organisation and enhance effectiveness.

## Managing risks and expectations

Supervising a complex sector where access to safely managed services is low, Sunass oversees a large and heterogeneous mix of providers that are often characterised by poor financial sustainability and a lack of compliance culture.

The attribution of new functions and an expansion of the scope of the regulator's remit to cover small towns and rural areas attests to Sunass's sound reputation. However, this is an enormous undertaking and government policies have set ambitious targets for the water and sanitation sector. Its new responsibilities have absorbed much of the regulator's attention as it strives to implement them by 2022, the deadline set in legislation. This task has been made even more challenging by an unstable political context and the disruption caused by the COVID-19 pandemic.

### *Key recommendations*

- As an independent regulator, assess and engage with stakeholders on risks linked to the delivery on new responsibilities and manage expectations for implementation, in a context of reduced resources and an ongoing pandemic.
- Review the delivery of Sunass functions to prioritise essential activities and ensure sufficient resources towards improving the performance of urban providers.

## Ensuring a fit-for-purpose regulatory toolbox

Sunass's functions include inspecting regulated entities, setting tariffs, issuing regulations, sanctioning operators and resolving conflicts and claims. Its benchmarking of providers creates a powerful tool to incentivise sector performance and the regulator is improving its use of regulatory impact assessments.

Nevertheless, the regulator's functions, powers and tools do not always match the needs and characteristics of the sector, which include poor performance and a resistance among consumers to pay tariffs. The regulator has few tools for encouraging better performance, and 38% of urban water utilities have had their management temporarily taken over by a technical state agency, which could affect the longer-term capacity of the sector. Monetary sanctions are mostly ineffective in changing operator behaviour.

### Key recommendations

- Ensure a fit-for-purpose "toolbox" that incentivises behaviour change and takes into account sector challenges and specificities, including risk-based and behaviourally informed approaches.
- Increase the added-value of stakeholder engagement through targeted communication strategies and empowered and representative user councils.
- Make full use of benchmarking data for easy-to-understand guidance on interpreting key performance indicators that can help consumers hold operators to account.

## Consolidating the institutional transformation

Sunass has responded to its new responsibilities and expanded mandate by launching a significant institutional transformation. It can be commended for establishing its 24 decentralised offices in a short period of time. The transformation has the potential of increasing the regulator's effectiveness by bringing it closer to local operators, consumers and partners.

Sunass continues to develop capacity in the decentralised offices as it progressively delegates functions away from headquarters. Consistency in practices across offices will be important for impact and predictability in regulatory delivery. However, protocols for centralised communications along hierarchical lines may hinder this process.

### Key recommendations

- Update the "Sunass identity and culture" of an independent economic regulator across headquarters and the decentralised offices.
- Provide training to develop the expertise of staff in decentralised offices and increase the level of interaction among staff members across offices to exchange information and ensure consistency in the execution of regulatory activities.

## Collaborating and ensuring co-ordination

Sunass has established itself as a key actor for co-ordination at the sub-national level, and many actors report that it is an open and collaborative partner. Sunass involves municipal-level authorities (ATMs) in the engagement with rural providers. The ATMs perform a crucial role with the potential to increase the regulator's reach towards all rural providers.

However, a large number of institutions are involved in delivering sector policy objectives and there are no appropriate mechanisms for high-level co-ordination. A lack of role clarity hinders the achievement of sector objectives.

### Key recommendations

- Advocate for the creation of institutionalised, regular meetings for high-level co-ordination among all public authorities in the water and sanitation sector, to improve transparency, clarify roles and build a shared vision for the sector and trust among institutions.
- Join efforts in areas where the achievement of Sunass's strategic objectives and sectoral policy goals depend on the actions of other public authorities, for example in inspections.
- Promote data sharing and collective data collection with other public bodies in the sector.

# 1 Assessment and recommendations

This chapter summarises the main findings and recommendations of the Performance Assessment Framework for Economic Regulators (PAFER) review of Peru's water and sanitation services regulator, Sunass (*Superintendencia Nacional de Servicios de Saneamiento*). The recommendations aim to strengthen the regulator's organisational performance and governance structures and are divided into short, medium and longer term actions.

## Introduction

The National Superintendency of Sanitation Services *(Superintendencia Nacional de Servicios de Saneamiento,* Sunass) is Peru's economic regulator for sanitation services that includes drinking water, sewerage treatment and sanitary disposal of excreta. Created in 1992, it is one of four economic sector regulators in Peru.

**An ambitious and technically sound regulator, Sunass needs to manage risks and expectations about what can be achieved in a challenging national and sector context.** Government policies and plans have set ambitious targets for sanitation. In 2016, a new framework law for the sector expanded the scope of the regulator's remit to include the regulation and oversight of service providers in small cities and rural areas and added a number of additional functions. Most recently, the COVID-19 pandemic has created further disruption. As an independent regulator and technical expert on the sector, Sunass is well positioned to assess and communicate how and which policy goals can be achieved in the short, medium and long term.

**Going forward, the regulator has to ensure a fit-for-purpose toolbox that incentivises behaviour change by operators and consumers to address sector performance.** The regulator can build on its expertise and knowledge by, for example, increasing the use of behaviourally-informed tools and interventions, more risk-based approaches, as well as considering updating the design of the tariff model. Such initiatives could enhance incentives for sector performance and increase Sunass's impact.

**Sunass has responded to its new responsibilities by launching a significant institutional transformation that must now be consolidated.** The regulator has responded to its new mandate by creating 24 regional offices. This is seen as a positive move and has the potential to improve the effectiveness of Sunass by bringing it closer to operators and consumers throughout the territory. Going forward, in this new organisational model, the regulator needs to consolidate its institutional culture and ensure coherence in approaches. This will require continuing to build up the capacity of decentralised offices, and ensuring fluid communication and knowledge exchange between teams in headquarters and the regions.

**Ultimately, the urgent task of increasing access to safe drinking water and sanitation services requires coherent action and co-ordination among actors.** A large number of public authorities intervene in the water and sanitation sector at national and sub-national levels. For example, better data sharing and accessibility have been highlighted as specific needs for more effective public action for the sector. Sunass is a strong institutional actor in the sector in terms of its technical capacity, providing the potential to catalyse change and give useful inputs to the policymaking process, but greater role clarity is needed to realise this potential.

## Role and objectives

### *Mandate*

**A recent legislative reform has fundamentally transformed the role of Sunass from serving only main urban areas to covering the entire national territory.** For the first 25 years after its founding in 1992, Sunass regulated Peru's 50 municipal utilities *(Empresas Prestadoras del Servicio de Saneamiento,* EPs) that serve the country's larger urban areas. In 2016, the Framework Law for the Management and Provision of Sanitation Services (referred to from now on as Framework Law 1280) expanded the scope of the regulator's remit to include the supervision of 450 operators in small cities and more than 25 000 service providers in rural areas to ensure service quality and financial sustainability, in addition to on-going work with the 50 EPs. It also gave the regulator a number of additional functions. Framework Law 1280 defines Sunass's high-level objectives to "guarantee users the provision of sanitation services, in urban and rural areas, under quality conditions, in order to contribute to the health of the population and the preservation of the environment". The regulator works to achieve these objectives by setting tariffs, issuing regulations and supervising the provision of sanitation services by providers, and is recognised as an independent, technical expert on the sector.

**The expansion of the regulator's scope to small towns and rural areas is a massive undertaking that will require Sunass to carefully manage expectations about what can be achieved in the short, medium and longer term.** Following the 2016 reform, Sunass is responsible for the supervision of a heterogeneous mix of thousands of service providers with different capacities, coverage, types of network connections, and local contexts. Importantly, this sets Sunass apart from most water regulators globally (OECD, 2021[1]). Many operators, including among those historically regulated by Sunass, fail to meet basic standards of financial sustainability and sector performance is generally poor. Outcomes are alarming: according to data on Sustainable Develop Goal 6 (UN-Water, 2020[2]), access to at least basic service provision is 93% for drinking water and 79% for sanitation in Peru; access to services that are safely managed is lower at 51% for drinking water and 53% for sanitation. These figures also hide a stark rural-urban divide. A large informal sector – including many unregistered and unlicensed service providers – limits regulatory reach. This is compounded by attempts at political interference in rate-setting at the local level (Felgendreher and Lehmann, 2015[3]). The new responsibilities have absorbed much of the regulator's attention as it strives to implement them by 2022, the deadline set in legislation.

**The disruption caused by the COVID-19 pandemic has made the task even more challenging.** Restrictions on travel have made it difficult to engage with new stakeholders throughout the country's rural areas. The regulator has responded by switching many activities online (e.g. offering virtual trainings to rural providers, holding videoconferences for consumers) but these tools are not accessible to all, especially vulnerable consumers in remote and rural areas. In general, resources have been prioritised to responding to the sanitary emergency at the expense of some planned activities. The pandemic has also left the sector further weakened. EPs were permitted to use their reserve funds to respond to the sanitary emergency (for example, to provide off-grid solutions to guarantee access to water for hand washing). With funds depleted, questions of financial sustainability and resilience to any future shock come to the fore.

*Recommendations*

Short term:

- **Assess and engage with stakeholders** on risks linked to the delivery on new responsibilities and manage expectations as the 2022 deadline for implementation approaches, in a context of reduced resources and the COVID-19 pandemic. As an independent regulator and technical expert on the sector, Sunass is well-positioned to assess how achievable policy goals are in the short, medium and long term. Sunass could:

  o Monitor performance, in particular, in implementing the new responsibilities and functions. The regulator needs to assess what is working well and what is not leading to desired outcomes in terms of changing the behaviour of operators or consumers, as well as broader sector outcomes including service access, water quality and financial sustainability.

  o Make clear the potential trade-off between network expansion and improvements to service quality in the context of scarce investment resources and clearly communicate the regulator's approach to managing this trade-off.

  o Communicate risks clearly to key stakeholders and the wider public and develop scenarios that indicate which goals can be achieved in the short, medium and long term, and engage with stakeholders on these scenarios with the aim of agreeing joint goals and objectives for the sector.

- **Update** Sunass' identity, vision and mission to maintain a common sense of purpose for staff internally and communicate a clear message to external stakeholders, to reflect the new responsibilities and functions that Sunass has taken on in recent years and the institutional transformation that took place.

Medium term:

- **Match** the reform of Sunass's role and scope of action with a consolidation of the drive for institutional transformation, using the new identity and vision statement as a guide.
    - Keep under review the capacity, competencies and powers of Sunass. These have already evolved as a consequence of the expansion of the regulator's scope and functions. Sunass will need to keep these under review in light of its performance in delivering on its new responsibilities.

### *Functions and powers*

**The regulator's functions, powers and tools do not always match the needs and characteristics of the sector, such as resistance to paying tariffs.** The Framework Law for Regulatory Bodies (*Ley marco de los organismos reguladores de la inversión privada en los servicios públicos*, Law 27332, or LMOR) grants Sunass, as with all Peruvian sector regulators, the functions to supervise, set tariffs, issue regulations, inspect the activity of regulated entities, sanction operators, and solve conflicts and claims. Nevertheless, overall sector performance is poor and the regulator has few tools that can incentivise better performance. Nineteen out of the 50 EPs are under the "Transitional Support Regime" due to poor performance, in which the Technical Organisation for the Administration of Sanitation Services (*Organismo Técnico de la Administración de los Servicios de Saneamiento,* OTASS) assumes management control of the utility. More broadly, there is significant resistance to paying for water services and therefore to implementing tariff decisions. As a result, tariffs are not set at a sufficient level to contribute to investment in upgrading and expanding infrastructure. Given the huge investment needed to meet national goals for access to water and sanitation, Sunass's tariff-setting function is central to successful performance.

**The attribution of new functions attests to Sunass's reputation as a technically sound agency but the regulator will need to carefully allocate resources towards sector priority goals.** Recent reforms bestow Sunass with a number of new tasks that go beyond the core regulatory functions shared by all sector regulators in Peru. New responsibilities include defining the geographical area that utilities must serve and promoting Mechanisms of Rewards for Ecosystem Services (*Mecanismos de Retribución por servicios Ecosistémicos,* MERESE), among others. Sunass has invested significant energy and resources to deliver the new functions and has gained recognition as a "strategic ally" by other public institutions for its efforts. However, among Sunass's numerous functions, it will also be important to continue incentivising performance of the 50 EPs that serve the country's larger urban areas. In this area a considerable number of challenges remain: to enable and provide incentives to EPs to improve their financial performance and to address quality of service provision issues such as drops in water pressure, contamination and a lack of access to drinking water and sanitation services. This should result in better overall outcomes for consumers.

**The transition to a new tariff-setting model requires a gradual transition process based on realistic expectations.** Currently, tariff increases are linked to the achievement of regulatory objectives. The regulator is in the process of introducing an "adapted" model company approach to tariff setting, as stipulated in Framework Law 1280. In this transition, care should be taken to avoid dramatic changes while moving from a cost-based approach to the new model. During this transition, revenue requirements should move in line with realistic improvements in operations, and collections need to yield cash flows that enable operators to reach regulatory targets in terms of connections and service quality (improving water pressure and reducing leaks and commercial losses).

*Recommendations*

Short term:

- **Review** the approach to the delivery of Sunass functions to prioritise essential activities. For example, Sunass could consider delimiting its role in the MERESE scheme to that which is strictly necessary in the process (e.g. the tariff calculation component). Explore the possibilities of identifying other institutions better placed to support EPs in the investment of MERESE funds in upstream river basins.

- **Ensure** a fit-for-purpose "toolbox", taking into account sector challenges and specificities, and focus on the outcome of behaviour change (Box 1.1).

  o Continue the good practice of making tariff increases conditional on the achievement of regulatory objectives (such as service quality, compliance with investment programme). Communicate on whether the targets have been reached, and how this affects the tariff.

  o Be realistic when designing the adapted model company approach for tariff setting. Favour an approach that provides a number of easy to understand and intuitive cost benchmarks based on comparable firms, rather than a highly technical analysis that requires detailed information on efficient operating costs for each individual EP.

  o Adopt a risk-based and behaviourally-informed approach to enforcement and inspections (see section on Regulatory enforcement and inspections).

  o Recognise, award and share good practice by different actors, e.g. a competition to award the best performing Municipal Technical Area (*Áreas Técnicas Municipales* – ATM), as well as service providers.

  o Equip consumers with the information they need to hold their water utilities to account for their performance. Clear, easy-to-understand trends in key performance indicators can show consumers whether service is improving or deteriorating. This could have an important repercussion on their willingness to pay higher tariffs.

  o Implement targeted communication strategies to reach different groups of important stakeholders:

    – Assign sufficient budget to design targeted consumer outreach campaigns (Box 1.2).

    – Initiate more regular contact with Congress and facilitate discussion around the annual report.

    – Build the media as an ally for communicating on the role of the regulator and its view on sector issues. Building an understanding of Sunass' role and on-going initiatives among the media could facilitate the sharing of Sunass opinions on sector issues and increase media coverage beyond its focus on when things go wrong.

Medium term:

- **Ensure** sufficient resources dedicated to improving the performance of the 50 EPs. Although Sunass has been given new responsibilities, it should continue to dedicate an appropriate level of its resources towards the on-going economic regulation of utilities that serve the country's larger urban areas. In this effort, Sunass should make sure to implement the new tariff model gradually, based on realistic expectations of the ability of EPs to improve operations and quality (Box 1.3).

- **Recognise and stress** the long-term impact of improving sewerage and wastewater services for water quality, the environment, and public health. It would be important to develop a realistic medium term strategy for investing in treatment plants and maintaining their operating efficiency. This effort should not be conducted solely by Sunass, but should include the other actors who would play a role in financing those facilities and monitoring water resource quality.

**Box 1.1. Institutional transformation to deliver on a modified regulatory framework in the Scottish water sector**

During its most recent price review process (the Strategic Review of Charges 2021-27, or SRC21), the Water Industry Commission for Scotland (WICS) saw an opportunity to address key challenges in the sector: a perceived adversarial approach in regulation, challenges with long-life assets, lack of flexibility of investment, and challenges of embedding consumer voices. The result was a modified regulatory framework that represents a radical change from the Scottish water sector status quo.

The state-owned monopoly provider in the household market, Scottish Water, faces the challenge of transforming what has been a delivery institution into a company embracing the principles of the modified regulatory framework. The company agreed to produce a transformation plan, with an aim of transforming decision making and cultural practice from top to bottom.

WICS created an additional layer of accountability in the company's production of its transformation plan. It asked a group of citizens convened to relay customer views into the price setting process, the Customer Forum, to engage with Scottish Water on its transformation plan. After discussions, Scottish Water and the Customer Forum entered into a minute of agreement on expectations for the transformation plan. The company launched its transformation planning with a stock-take of its company character and is working with experts and a management consultancy as it develops a transformation plan.

WICS has taken the first steps in its own transformation planning, reflecting on necessary adjustments through expert workshops and in its corporate plan. The two institutions have worked together on certain aspects of transformation planning, such as joint sessions on enacting Ethical Business Regulation (a key feature of the modified regulatory framework).

In light of the scale of institutional change required, demonstrable progress towards organisational transformation will be important to build confidence that parties are making necessary organisational changes to meet the challenges ahead. During SRC21, WICS created an Ethical Business Regulation Support Group to provide a regular "temperature check" of EBR principles such as trust and openness during SRC21. The support group conducted assessments via regular anonymous online surveys and face-to-face interviews of the parties involved in SRC21, providing an analysis with recommendations after each assessment. The support group provides one example of a mechanism to help parties recalibrate as they adjust their approaches and ways of working in the context of organisational transformation and regulatory framework change, and parties will continue to consider how to provide reassurance that the company and regulatory framework are delivering.

Source: Information provided by the Water Industry Commission for Scotland, 2021.

**Box 1.2. Consumer empowerment and information to the consumer provided by Portugal's Energy Services Regulatory Authority (ERSE)**

As part of its mission to protect energy consumer rights and interests, ERSE seeks to empower energy consumers by informing them of their rights and how they can make informed choices, through a variety of tools:

- Dedicated website for consumers
- Online comparison tools on energy offers, contracted power and the origin of their energy
- Multimedia materials on energy issues
- Outreach activities (radio, television, print media, school visits)
- Capacity-building activities (onsite and virtual training courses)
- Telephone hotline to answer consumer queries and complaints
- Dispute resolution and mediation and support to public arbitration centres

ERSE's website has a dedicated area for consumers. Consumers can find a full range of information in multiple formats regarding ERSE's regulated sectors, such as alerts on bad practices, tips, comparison tools, videos explaining how the sectors work, as well as data and statistics. The website also provides information explaining the right to and procedures for dispute resolution, including ERSE's role in this regard. In this area "Gia", an online virtual assistant is available that answers consumer questions through a chat box.

However, not all consumers have digital access or competence to consult this array of online information. Only through the diversification of direct and indirect information channels is it possible to reach a multiplicity of target audiences with different degrees of literacy, education, age groups and locations. With this in mind, ERSE also provides a dedicated telephone assistance service for the public, available between 15:00 and 18:00 on working days, as well as a face-to-face service, by prior appointment.

In addition, the need to reach less informed audiences requires a more active intervention and investing in new means of communication. Consequently, ERSE decided to broadcast paid information campaigns on the radio to reach an older audience. ERSE is also invited to attend informative news programmes in order to reach energy consumers, for example to explain energy tariffs and bills. Some recordings are also available on ERSE's YouTube Channel. ERSE does not pay for or receive remuneration for attending such programmes.

ERSE is working to diversify further its means of communication with energy consumers, including: cooperating with the National Guard to visit schools, retirement centres and others to inform about energy, increased social media presence, using plain language in its publications and subscribing to online banner services on news aggregation websites, for example.

ERSE also organises training sessions, aimed mainly at consumer associations and arbitration centres for consumer disputes, and participates in events organised by other entities in order to explain the functioning of energy markets, and in particular prices, bills and consumer rights.

Source: Information provided by ERSE, 2021.

---

**Box 1.3. Extending the coverage of regulation to a highly fragmented water industry: the approach of Italy's Authority for Energy, Networks and Environment (ARERA)**

The Authority for Energy, Networks and Environment (ARERA) is Italy's independent economic regulator for the water sector. Its regulation applies to water and wastewater services including the abstraction, supply and distribution of water for domestic use, sewerage and wastewater treatment, as well as extraction, multi-purpose water supply and treatment services for mixed residential and industrial use.

## A fragmented water industry

The water industry in Italy is highly fragmented with more than 2 000 operators providing water, sewerage and wastewater treatment services to a total population of 60 million. The vast majority of operators are municipal operators in the south of the country, while in the central and northern areas around 100 medium to large operators serve more than 80% of the population. A few large, multi-sector utilities have a market share of more than 50%.

## Governance framework

According to legislation, the Ministry of Environment defines the general principles of water use and services at the national level while ARERA provides the specific rules, mechanisms and procedures and ensures compliance. Regions set the geographical area to which integrated water services must be provided (*Ambito Territoriale Ottimale*, ATO) and identify the local authority (the EGA, generally a regional or sub-regional entity) which is in charge of organising integrated water services at the local level, planning investments and contracting the management of services to operators through public tendering or concessions. Water services may be provided in an integrated way by a single operator or separately by different operators.

## Extending the coverage of regulation

Several hundred operators (mainly municipalities directly managing water services in southern Italy) have not yet obtained a tariff approval from ARERA in accordance with the national tariff methodology, as they have not submitted the required information to the regulator. In order to extend the coverage of regulation to these operators progressively, ARERA launched a simplified tariff methodology (the "convergence tariff methodology") for the 2020-2023 tariff period. This provides a facilitated tariff approval procedure for operators that lack data on revenues, costs and quality of service provision. An operator or the EGA can estimate allowed revenues through the approach defined in the methodology, which provides simplified procedures for tariff planning. Thanks to this approach, in 2021 the EGA of the Calabria region submitted its first tariff plan on behalf of several municipalities in the region. This was an important initial step toward the progressive inclusion of the smallest water providers under the umbrella of regulation.

In addition to this bottom up approach, ARERA signalled the need for legislative reform of water governance in the south to the national government and to the parliament in order to accelerate the transfer of responsibility for providing water services to utilities. ARERA suggested to mandatorily entrust responsibility for water services to publicly-owned companies in cases where EGAs were not able to carry out public procedures to select an operator.

Source: Information provided by the Italian Authority for Energy, Networks and Environment (ARERA), 2021.

## *Strategic framework*

**The regulator's strategic plan provides a solid framework for performance assessment, which could be further strengthened by inviting inputs from external stakeholders.** Sunass operates in the framework of a five-year strategic plan (PEI) that identifies a balanced set of strategic objectives that span input, process, output and outcome measures (Table 1.1). Sunass' external stakeholders (such as its Users Councils), however, are not consulted during the strategic planning process, which is a missed opportunity. Including external stakeholders in the process would have the additional benefit of increasing understanding of the regulator's role and strengthening water governance more broadly.

**Strategic planning needs to balance agility with predictability.** Changes to the strategic plan are allowed by legislation during strategic cycles but these should be predictable and not undermine stability of the regulator's priorities. Frequent reviews might create ambiguities about the regulator's priorities for staff and stakeholders. In this context, developing an overarching vision and institutional values could help to provide a longer-term horizon to the work of the regulator.

### Table 1.1. Sunass strategic objectives analysed according to OECD input-process-output-outcome framework

Sunass's strategic objectives as part of its strategic plan (PEI) 2020-24

| Objective (OEI) | Type of objective |
| --- | --- |
| 1. Strengthen the provision of sanitation services to users | OUTCOME |
| 2. Consolidate the decentralisation of Sunass functions | PROCESS |
| 3. Improve the perception and appreciation of sanitation services by users | OUTCOME |
| 4. Strengthen Institutional Management | INPUT |
| 5. Implement disaster risk management* | OUTPUT |

\* This objective is mandatory for all public bodies, as set by the National Centre for Strategic Planning (*Centro Nacional de Planeamiento Estratégico*, CEPLAN).
Source: Information provided by Sunass, 2021.

*Recommendations*

Short term:

- **Use** the strategic plan as a tool to manage risks and expectations by closely monitoring and reporting on the delivery of strategic objectives.
- **Consult** stakeholders as part of the strategic planning process. For example, Sunass could consider:
  - Organising public consultations through Sunass decentralised offices.
  - Seeking the opinion of its Users Councils.
  - Using existing platforms for citizen engagement such as the Participa vecino! initiative.
  - Going the extra mile to include the perspectives of unserved populations and vulnerable consumers.
  - Clearly communicating the final strategic plan using the same channels as the consultation process, and reach a wider public through the regulator's website, newsletter, and the media. Sunass could also consider organising a launch event to raise awareness and give visibility. Using plain language and translating into local languages can help ensure accessibility.

Medium term:

- **Increase** predictability in the strategic planning process and signal the regulator's longer-term direction of travel. Greater stability from the regulator is particularly important in the context of political instability.
  - Pre-define and communicate from the outset when Sunass will carry out a mid-term review of the strategic plan.
  - Explain clearly the rationale for any changes to the strategic objectives or goals.
  - Include stakeholder consultation in the review.
  - Develop a vision statement that signals the regulator's longer-term priorities for the sector, beyond the 3-5 year institutional planning cycle.

*Institutional co-ordination*

**A lack of role clarity between different public actors hinders the achievement of sector objectives.** Overall, there is a mismatch between the complex legal framework for the water and sanitation sector and the capacity of Peru's institutions to implement it (OECD, 2021[1]). Low capacity contributes to and is compounded by a lack of clarity around roles and responsibilities. For Sunass, this has resulted in a mismatch between the role it performs and the expectations of other public sector actors. For example, there are expectations that Sunass should ensure that service providers deliver drinking water that meets required safety standards. However, responsibility for monitoring drinking water quality lies with the Health Authority (DIGESA). Nevertheless, poor water quality may undermine popular acceptance of tariffs, essential to the successful delivery of Sunass's mandate. Users and communities expect access to quality public services with little concern for which public institutions are responsible, hence the importance for all actors to work together and share ownership of common goals.

**Despite the number of institutions involved in delivering sector policy objectives, appropriate mechanisms for high-level co-ordination are not in place.** Framework Law 1280 defines the respective roles of the large number of ministries and other public bodies that intervene sector, including Sunass, as well as local and regional governments and service providers. Under this legislative framework, the Ministry of Housing, Construction and Sanitation (MVCS) is the governing body for sanitation and has exclusive power over the development, planning, co-ordination, implementation and oversight of national specific and related policies. Beyond definitions in law, there are no regular, institutionalised meetings for co-ordination between public authorities in the sector.

**In a context of overlap and weak institutional capacity, Sunass has sometimes taken action to tackle existing or emerging problems beyond its functions as defined in legislation.** Many actors report that Sunass is an open, collaborative and dynamic partner. In some instances, in order to support providers' performance, the regulator steps in where it identifies gaps or other actors are not able to fulfil their role. For example, Sunass carries out training and capacity building activities in EPs and rural service providers, which may overlap with the role of the MVCS and its technical agency for the administration of sanitation services, OTASS.

**Sunass has established itself as a key actor for co-ordination at the sub-national level, but this remains a difficult task.** Sunass operates in a particularly complex institutional landscape in rural areas, with interventions from a large number of ministries as well as regional and municipal levels of government. The capacity of local actors is typically low. However, in some aspects, effective co-ordination appears to rely on the capacity of Sunass to be physically present in a locality and able to interact with municipal governments and service providers. Despite the positive development of its 24 regional offices, the relatively limited number of Sunass staff in these offices combined with the remote and difficult-to-access nature of many areas of the country may still hinder co-ordination.

**At the international level, Sunass is active in fora to promote international regulatory co-operation, and could turn to these networks more frequently to exchange on practices and regulatory approaches.** Sunass participates in the Association of Water and Sanitation Regulatory Bodies of the Americas (*Asociación de Entes Reguladores de Agua y Saneamiento de las Americas*, ADERASA) and other international and regional initiatives. As Sunass implements its new responsibilities, there could be value in strengthening engagement with other water regulators in the region to compare how sector regulation is organised in neighbouring countries. As these countries will operate in contexts that show similarities with the context of the Peruvian water sector, this could enable cross-learning on how fellow regulators have tackled common challenges.

*Recommendations*

Short term:

- **Advocate** for the creation of institutionalised, regular meetings for high-level co-ordination between all public authorities in the water and sanitation sector. In line with its mandate for whole-of-government co-ordination, the PCM could be well placed to convene heads of institutions on a regular basis (e.g. monthly, quarterly). Formalised and regular interactions can improve transparency and the flow of information, clarify roles and avoid duplication, and over time build a shared vision for the sector and trust between institutions.
- **Assess** where co-ordination mechanisms for regulatory practices are needed at different levels of government to clarify roles and responsibilities and optimise the efficient use of resources.
  - Consider co-ordination mechanisms such as agreements detailing respective roles, areas of co-operation, or electronic access to information held by other bodies.
- **Join efforts** in areas where the achievement of Sunass strategic objectives and sectoral policy goals depend on the actions of other actors. Areas to consider could be:
  - Water quality: co-ordinated inspections and enforcement actions with DIGESA could improve outcomes for consumers. Alternatively, Sunass may consider advocating for the transfer of some monitoring activities, where there is a case of overlap between different bodies.
  - The integration of smaller service providers into EPs: establish working groups with all relevant stakeholders in each region (sub-national governments, the EP and smaller providers, OTASS, consumer representatives) to discuss the results of Sunass proposed service delivery area.
  - "Transitional Support Regime": closer collaboration and discussion with OTASS around which EPs should enter the scheme.
  - Communication: Sunass could consider forming 'strategic coalitions' to communicate in simple terms about the rationale for paying for water or increasing tariffs. For example, coherent messaging from the regulator, MVCS, the Ministry of Health, the Ministry of Development and Social Inclusion and others could help strengthen the message that better quality water services can promote health and economic development.

Medium term:

- **Put in place** co-operation agreements at the sub-national level to empower local institutions to carry out certain regulatory functions. For example, to leverage the 'on the ground' presence of municipal governments, Sunass could authorise ATM staff to carry out monitoring and inspection functions in rural areas beyond the period currently envisaged. The division of roles would need to be clearly communicated to rural service providers and other stakeholders.
- **Continue and strengthen** regional co-operation on water regulation (Box 1.4). Sunass could explore the potential within ADERASA or other regional fora to increase the level of interaction to:
  - exchange experiences, good practices and solutions to common problems;
  - enable regional comparisons of regulatory practices and approaches through surveys and data sharing; and
  - build capacity in its members, for example through seminars, trainings or by establishing or associating with a school of regulation.
  - In these efforts, the capacity of regional associations could be strengthened through international development financing.

---

**Box 1.4. International co-ordination and co-operation between regulatory agencies: the ARIAE experience**

The Ibero-American Association of Energy Regulatory Entities (Asociación Iberoamericana de Entidades Reguladoras de la Energía, ARIAE) brings together 27 energy regulatory authorities from 20 Ibero-American countries (Mexico, Portugal, Spain, Central American countries and Spanish- or Portuguese-speaking South American countries).

ARIAE is an association of energy regulators that constitutes a forum for communication between specialists and professionals of its member entities. Its purpose is to promote the exchange of experiences and knowledge in the field of energy regulation, promote regulatory harmonisation, promote the training and education of personnel belonging to its members, at all levels; as well as promoting co-operation in activities of common interest, including research and development. The association is also working to achieve universal access to modern energy sources in the region.

The systematic exchange of information and experiences is supported by the annual meetings of regulators, in the operation of their working groups (on electricity, gas, petroleum products, biofuels, upstream and consumers), their training activities and the elaboration of books and reports, and through the operation of their website and the daily publication of news on its social networks.

ARIAE is the promoter of the Ibero-American School of Energy Regulation (EIR), with two branches, one for the regulation of the electricity sector at the Pontificia Universidad Católica in Chile, and another for the regulation of the hydrocarbons sector at the ESAN University in Peru, with the participation in each of them, of a group of seven universities in the region and elsewhere.

ARIAE has the support of international development partners, such as the Spanish Agency for International Development Cooperation (AECID), the Ibero-American General Secretariat (SEGIB) and the Inter-American Development Bank (IDB). In addition, ARIAE has collaboration agreements with the Economic Commission for Latin America and the Caribbean (ECLAC), the Latin American Energy Organization (OLADE), the World Bank, the Andean Development Corporation (CAF), and the Latin American Association of Sustainable Mobility (ALAMOS).

Additionally, ARIAE holds regular meetings with other regional energy associations, and participates in the World Energy Regulation Forums organised by ICER.

The General Secretariat of ARIAE is managed by the National Commission of Markets and Competition of Spain (CNMC).

Source: Information provided by the National Commission of Markets and Competition of Spain (CNMC), 2021.

---

### Input into policy and law making

**In this big picture, full use isn't always made of Sunass' expertise for the benefit of sector policy and outcomes.** Sunass prepares non-binding opinions and comments when requested by the Congress of the Republic and ministries on proposed policies, laws and ministerial regulations; it lacks the power to submit binding opinions. Despite the strong technical capacity and its potential to provide valuable input into policy making, Sunass is not systematically consulted. On occasion, the regulator has proactively submitted comments when not requested. Finally, Sunass does not make public the comments and opinions it submits. This is a missed opportunity for improving transparency and safeguarding the independence of the regulator.

*Recommendations*

Short term:

- **Publish** Sunass opinions on its website and publicise them through traditional and social media to ensure transparency around its inputs into the policy-making process. Building good relations with the media could help them to stay alert to Sunass statements and afford them the necessary attention.

- **Catalogue** the opinions that Sunass emits in its annual report (Box 1.5).

- **Make full use** of Sunass's role as an independent regulator to raise red flags when necessary and to play a proactive role in placing important issues on the policy-making as well as public information agenda. While remaining a strategic and technical partner of the government, Sunass could take a more proactive stance towards Congress to raising issues and making its position known.

---

### Box 1.5. Publication of formal opinions by Portugal's Energy Services Regulatory Authority (ERSE)

Most of ERSE's opinions, studies, reports and memorandums prepared within the scope of the regulator's statutory obligations or regulatory procedures, as well as others prepared on its own initiative, or at the request of a third party, including the Government and the Assembly of the Republic, are published on ERSE's website. ERSE opinions are also published in its annual report.

ERSE's website has a dedicated online library that is a repository of relevant legislation and regulation for the sector as well as of ERSE's activities, including recommendations, opinions, ERSE's consultative councils, reports, bulletins, studies and memoranda. This library includes documents that ERSE is legally obliged to prepare and publish and serves as a platform for transparency and co-operation.

Without prejudice to requests for access or disclosure under legal terms, as a rule, the publication of these documents occurs at the first of the following moments: after a decision has been taken by the entity that requested ERSE's opinion; one year after the preparation of the ERSE document; within the legal deadline for publication (e.g. in annual reports).

The availability of such documents does not cover information that, by its nature, is commercially sensitive, constitutes a legally protected secret or personal data.

Whenever opinions/studies/reports/memoranda are part of an ongoing process by an external party, ERSE applies an internal process to identify when its document can be published, in line with the above considerations. For example, when the government requests an opinion from ERSE on a legislative proposal it is not disclosed immediately, but only after the respective government diploma is published in the Portuguese Official Journal, usually the same day or the next.

This measure safeguards the political decision-making debate. However, once the diploma is published, any stakeholder can check whether ERSE's opinion was included, partially included or not included at all. For greater transparency, the published opinions include a reference to when ERSE's input was requested by the third party.

Source: Information provided by ERSE, 2021.

---

## Input

### *Financial resources*

**The reform of Sunass's mandate changed the regulator's financing model, making government budget its main source of funding.** Prior to the expansion of its scope, Sunass was funded solely by fees from the EPs that it regulated, collecting a maximum of 1% of income after sales taxes. This cap, set in legislation for all economic regulators, was considered for increase to 2% by a congressional committee but the decision has not passed through Congress. Since 2017, government funds provide the majority of the budget (58% in 2021) (Table 1.2), representing a dramatic change in the regulator's funding model and subjecting it to uncertainty regarding its budget. Government funds are intended to cover the expansion of supervision to small cities and rural areas.

### Table 1.2. Sunass sources of revenue, 2015-2020

| Source of revenue | 2015 | | 2016 | | 2017 | | 2018 | | 2019 | | 2020 | | 2021 | | 2022 (est.) | |
|---|---|---|---|---|---|---|---|---|---|---|---|---|---|---|---|---|
| | PEN mln | % of total | PEN mln | % of total | PEN mln | % of total | PEN mln | % of total | PEN mln | % of total | PEN mln | % of total | PEN mln | % of total | PEN mln | % of total |
| Government funds | 0 | 0 | 0 | 0 | 27.9 | 48 | 52.7 | 66 | 64.1 | 61 | 68.5 | 65 | 55.5 | 58 | 53.1 | 63 |
| Fees | 27.8 | 100 | 29.8 | 100 | 30.8 | 52 | 27.4 | 34 | 41.1 | 39 | 37.2 | 35 | 40.3 | 42 | 31.2 | 37 |
| Resources from Official Credit Operations | 0 | 0 | 0 | 0 | 0 | 0 | 0 | 0 | 0 | 0 | 0.2 | 0 | 0 | 0 | 0 | 0 |
| Total | 27.8 | 100 | 29.8 | 100 | 58.6 | 100 | 80.1 | 100 | 105.2 | 100 | 105.9 | 100 | 95.8 | 100 | 84.3 | 100 |

Source: Information provided by Sunass, 2021.

**Relatively low fees from regulated entities combined with uncertainty and significant cuts in government funding could undermine the stability of the regulator and threaten to reduce its autonomy.** Before the expansion of its scope of action, Sunass considered that its budget was inadequate to carry out its functions fully, as water utilities in Peru tend to be small public utilities with low business income. As a result, its income from fees was considerably smaller than the other sector regulators in Peru (see (OECD, 2019[4]) (OECD, 2019[5]) (OECD, 2020[6])).[1] Moreover, the sustainability of funding from government funds is uncertain given fiscal consolidation efforts. The budget decreased by 10% to PEN 95.8 million in 2021, and is expected to decrease by another 12% to PEN 84 million in 2022. The lack of stability in financing risks undermining the regulator's ability to adequately plan activities, carry out its functions fully and meet its goals, thereby reducing its effectiveness and autonomy.

**The regulator's current planning and budgeting processes are not sufficient to withstand these challenges.** Sunass establishes multi-annual budget estimates that are designed to respond to such challenges, but in practice the government approves the budget on an annual basis. The multi-annual budgeting process fails to serve the purpose of establishing medium-term budget certainty. Sunass responds to budget cuts by revising down goals while continuing to deliver across all areas. This approach may not be realistic or desirable in terms of improving outcomes in the sector, which could be best served through a realistic prioritisation of activities, goals and expectations.

**Sunass's ability to manage its resources autonomously is in some cases constrained by central government requirements.** Government funds are earmarked for activities in rural areas and small towns. However, as some personnel carry out functions in both urban and rural areas these funds are difficult to isolate for allocation purposes. Other recently introduced government requirements include the obligation to return any budget surpluses to the Treasury every year.

*Recommendations*

Short term:

- **Devise** a strategic response to foreseen budget cuts that makes clear the risks associated with budget shortfalls. As an independent regulator, Sunass is in a position to:
    - Advocate for adequate planning and resources for the sector due to its key role in any response to and recovery from the COVID-19 pandemic. The pandemic underscored the importance of water and sanitation for health and the economy. Sunass could use this moment to elevate water and sanitation in the public policy-making agenda.
    - Prioritise objectives and identify which activities and deliverables would need to be cancelled in the event of significant budget shortfall.
    - Introduce a risk-proportionality approach when prioritising to ensure a focus on the higher risk-related activities in case of insufficient budget to deliver all planned activities.
    - Develop evidence on the impact of budget cuts on outcomes for consumers, for example: a budget cut of "x" PEN will result in unmonitored water services for "y" population, increasing risks to public health: incidents of diseases linked to untreated water could be expected to increase by "z"%.
    - Present and clearly communicate to key stakeholders (MVCS, PCM, MEF and Congress) to demonstrate what the regulator can deliver given the level of resourcing and the consequences in terms of outcomes for the sector.

Medium term:

- **Advocate** for budget setting according to an estimation of the costs of regulating and supervising the sector, rather than available resources. This could be used as a basis for discussion and negotiation on the budget with the executive and strengthen the regulator's case for more resources and flexibility. In case efficient costs of running the regulator exceed revenues, Sunass could advocate for raising the cap on fees (Box 1.6).
- **Continue** the good practice of multi-annual budgeting and use this as the primary tool in the annual budget negotiation and approval process. Make transparent and public when the approved annual budget deviates significantly from the multi-annual budget plan.
- **Advocate** for great autonomy in managing financial resources: for example, end the earmarking of funds; carry over unspent resources from one budget year to the next.

Long term:

- **Work** towards a vision in which tariffs are set at levels that enable all operators to be in good financial health, thereby enabling adequate financing of the regulator through fees. This vision could support a discussion on the potential need for subsidies and/or the design of cross-subsidies where cost-reflective tariffs are not compatible with the affordability of services for vulnerable consumers. In a well-performing sector, revenues from fees could become the majority of the regulator's funding.

---

**Box 1.6. Ensuring cost-recovery appropriately supports the regulator, in the short- and medium-term**

**Latvia's Public Utilities Commission (PUC)**

As a consequence of a legislative change in 2017, the regulatory fee that funds the PUC's operations is set directly in legislation. To account for any potential overpayments above the PUC's budget as approved by Parliament, excess funds are deposited in the account of the regulator at the Treasury.

---

These limited funds can serve also to avoid unexpected or transitory decrease in PUC's income without revising primary legislation every year.

The regulator can use these funds to fund its operations in subsequent years, in accordance with its approved budget. In case the funds in the account exceed 25% of total fee revenues, the excess funds are returned to market operators through a deduction in fee payments in the respective year.

### Ireland's Commission for Regulation of Utilities (CRU)

The CRU is funded entirely through levy and licence fees from relevant electricity, gas, petroleum safety, and water industry participants. Levies from market participants comprise the bulk of the CRU's income. The CRU sets its own budget without requiring government participation, and is defined annually on a cost-recovery basis in the fourth quarter of the year, on the basis of an estimate of CRU operating and capital budget required for the next year. There is no direct government contribution to the CRU budget and the regulator's annual budget is approved by the Commission without approval or ex ante assessment by the Oireachtas.

Annual budgets for the electricity, gas, petroleum and water are allocated by the CRU to each sector. Revenues, expenses and capital expenditure directly incurred by each sector are recorded in the separate budgets of the electricity, gas, petroleum and water sectors. Shared costs are allocated to each sector in proportion to the staff numbers engaged in the relevant sector. Costs linked to shared administrative functions such as finance, HR, IT, and communications are pooled for all sectors.

Where annual expenditures exceed revenue, the balance is offset against the levy income for the subsequent year. The balances for the electricity, gas, petroleum and water sectors are recorded in their respective accounts, and audited on an annual basis by the Office of the Comptroller and Auditor General, which reports to the Public Accounts Committee of the Oireachtas. The CRU also conducts an annual internal audit, which is outsourced to an audit company. Moreover, based on a risk assessment, a contingency fund is defined on a yearly basis to provide flexibility to deal with potential legal challenges or costs linked to safety cases or events. Any excess of revenue in the financial year is taken into account in determining the levy for the subsequent year per sector. The CRU can carry unspent funds over to the following year's budget without review or approval from external government entities.

### Canada Energy Regulator (CER)

The CER's Cost Recovery Regulations set out the manner in which the CER determines the costs related to carrying out its mandate and the process for recovering all or a portion of those costs from the companies it regulates. Currently, the CER's cost recovery system is premised on commodity charging costs that are allocated to specific entities within those sectors (oil – oil pipelines, gas – gas pipelines, etc.). The CER performs the administrative functions of calculating, billing and collecting cost recovery levies from industry on behalf of the Government of Canada –it does not have re-spendable revenue authority. Instead, companies pay their share of recoverable costs to the Consolidated Revenue Fund of Canada and the CER receives its funding through an annual appropriation process through Parliament.

The CER has a Cost Recovery Liaison Committee, which is composed of the staff from the regulator and representatives of the regulated companies. The purpose of this committee is to:

- provide industry with a thorough understanding of CER costs,
- provide a forum to raise issues or concerns related to the cost recovery processes and methods; and,
- discuss the Cost Recovery Regulations.

Source: Information provided by PUC, CRU and CER, 2021.

*Human resources*

**The regulator's workforce has been increasing as its scope and functions have expanded, but resources remain stretched given the urgent needs of the sector.** The staff of Sunass is competent and shares a common sense of purpose, but the regulator's level of ambition and new functions may mean that its workforce is reaching the limits of what it can deliver. The number of staff grew by nearly 25% between 2017 and 2020, however, several areas report being under-resourced. The internal audit office (OCI) confirms this assessment in the area of inspections. This could create frustration if staff cannot implement work plans.

**The profile of Sunass staff will need to evolve in step with its new responsibilities.** As well as recruiting local staff with expertise in regulatory functions such as inspection and supervision, Sunass's new functions require staff with different skillsets, taking into account soft skills as well as technical competencies, e.g. communications, skills to engage with different types of stakeholders, or to carry out capacity building in ATMs. Staff often develop skills on-the-job and the learning curve can be long. The issue of recruiting, retaining and replacing qualified staff in small cities outside of Lima may become more important moving forward. Moreover, women are currently under-represented at senior management level, accounting for just four out of 16 senior posts.

**Ensuring Sunass remains an attractive place to work will be key to retain the talent needed to deliver for the sector and perform well against new objectives.** Sunass salaries are competitive compared to the regulated sector, although lower than in other Peruvian sector regulators. Staff turnover is relatively high (Table 1.3) and there are limited opportunities for career progression due to rigidity of the civil service labour regime. Overall, Sunass needs to ensure adequate remuneration and benefits packages that can reward high performers.

**Efforts may be needed to build trust among staff regarding equal treatment.** The regulator needs to build back trust after issues with delayed payment of staff salaries, which resulted in a number of labour lawsuits. Moreover, over 40% of staff are in the decentralised offices and this proportion could grow further as more functions are delegated. Higher salaries for new recruits in the decentralised offices when compared to staff in headquarters could lead to tensions that obstruct constructive working relationships and the transfer of institutional knowledge and expertise.

**Table 1.3. Staff turnover, 2017-2020**

|  | 2017 | 2018 | 2019 | 2020 |
|---|---|---|---|---|
| Turnover % | 18 | 20 | 18 | 13 |

Source: Information provided by Sunass, 2021.

**As allowed by law and practised across the public administration, many senior management positions at Sunass are filled outside any public and competitive selection process.** Eighteen posts within Sunass – mainly senior management positions (i.e. Heads of Directorates/Offices) – are appointed under the "puestos de confianza" (positions of trust) modality. This practice, while allowed by law, may create a sense of lack of transparency in hiring and appointments. This form of hiring could also hinder continuity of practice and decision making at Sunass, as many senior management posts may change when new leadership arrives.

*Recommendations*

Short term:

- **Consolidate** the talent pool needed for Sunass' new mandate and responsibilities with a focus on recruitment and retention.
  - o Take a more proactive approach to securing and developing the skills required, in particular in local job markets. For example, Sunass could collaborate with universities to develop programmes on economic regulation (in conjunction with other Peruvian economic regulators) and water engineering specialisations.
  - o Introduce a broader benefit employment package to ensure that Sunass remains an attractive place to work with special focus on ensuring equal treatment across the workforce

Medium term:

- **Reward** high performance internally by continuing to develop non-monetary incentives. For example, Sunass could develop employee of the month awards, or offer further training opportunities to good performers.
- **Introduce** a selection process for "puestos de confianza" to ensure continuity and stability to regulatory decision making.
- **Implement** gender-sensitive recruitment practices to increase the representation of women at senior levels in the organisation.

### *Internal organisation and management*

**Capacity in the decentralised offices is being developed, but protocols for communications may hinder this process.** Sunass's 24 decentralised offices have progressively taken on more functions and the expectation is that this trend will continue. The decentralised offices face constraints in terms of limited resources and capacities that take time to build. Communications with headquarters are centralised hierarchically through the head of each decentralised office, who reports to the Service Area Directorate in Lima, as opposed to each specialist communicating with their colleagues in their technical area. Currently the decentralised offices receive guidelines and periodic trainings from their technical counterparts in headquarters (e.g. the Supervision Directorate), but do not have a direct channel of communication with them, which impedes knowledge exchange and fluid communications.

**With the expectation of more delegation to decentralised offices, consistency in practices between offices will be important for the effectiveness and predictability of regulatory delivery.** Sunass can be commended for establishing the decentralised offices in a short period of time and in the challenging context of the COVID-19 pandemic. Going forward, a sufficient level of interaction between the decentralised offices and Sunass's central office will be essential to align practices across offices, but also to learn from good practices regarding the execution of regulatory activities. To help standardise practices, Sunass already established macro-regions and periodic meetings between the heads of decentralised offices and senior management in headquarters, but no such meetings take place horizontally between teams. Sunass will have to consider how it can secure a need for consistency and predictability – to ensure equal treatment of regulated entities – without taking away the ability of decentralised offices to adjust practices according to local circumstances. It may not always be desirable to delegate all aspects of regulatory activities to the decentralised offices, as this could lead to inefficiencies for activities that require more specific expertise that the smaller offices cannot develop.

*Recommendations*

Short term:

- **Maintain** sufficient technical capacity at headquarters and update the Organisational Duties Regulation (*Reglamento de Organización y Funciones*, ROF) of specialised departments to oversee the methodology and quality of the work of the decentralised offices.

- **Develop** a roadmap for the delegation of functions to decentralised offices and clearly communicate it to all staff.
  - o Assess the costs and benefits related to the delegation of specific technical expertise and support functions, to ensure an efficient use of resources.
  - o Define a timeline and distribution of responsibilities for the delegation of activities. Factors to consider include existing and required capacities within decentralised offices, as well as risks that could affect the timeline.
- **Build** a coherent and consistent "Sunass identity and culture" as an independent economic regulator across headquarters and the decentralised offices. To achieve this, Sunass could consider:
  - o Increasing the level of interaction between the different offices to exchange information and good practices. More horizontal interaction (between technical staff working on similar topics across different offices) can help ensure consistency and support in the execution of regulatory activities. For example, Sunass could create communities of practice that bring together staff across from across the organisation (and from other public authorities and regulators) interested in particular topics, e.g. on supervision, communications for development, new technologies in sanitation etc. (Box 1.7).
  - o Continuing to build up the expertise of staff in decentralised offices through training and developing mechanisms to ensure transfer of knowledge and expertise from long-serving staff to newer recruits, in particular in decentralised offices.
  - o Ensuring consistency in approach across decentralised offices so that all parts of the organisation are operating in line with same organisational standards, codes and practices. Sunass may want to consider a matrix-structured organisation where different teams are grouped by function rather than by location. Additionally/alternatively, directorates in headquarters could have responsibility for providing guidance or granting final approval on work carried out in the decentralised offices.
  - o Facilitating exchanges of staff between headquarters and the decentralised offices, e.g. temporary placements of 3-6 months. This could help not only with transfer of knowledge and practices but could also safeguard against regulatory capture of decentralised offices. Shorter term exchanges, including for in-person training at headquarters or at the decentralised offices would also strengthen contacts, which could be very helpful for subsequent day-to-day consultation of colleagues in different locations.

---

**Box 1.7. Creating "Communities of Practice"**

Regulators have established communities of practice bringing together staff interested in particular topics as a way to share knowledge and stay abreast of latest developments.

**Communities of Practice at the Australian Competition and Consumer Commission (ACCC) and the Australian Energy Regulator (AER)**

The ACCC/AER has several internal communities of practice. For example, there is a community of practice on Communications & Engagement and another on Data Governance. The regulator also has internal networks which bring together like-minded people using specific tools or approaches. For example, there is a "Quantitative Analysis Network" that meets regularly to discuss and learn about tools and techniques for quantitative analysis (such as R, excel, python). An "Economics Network" meets to share issues and developments in economics.

---

---

**Professional Networks at Sweden's Post and Telecom Authority (PTS)**

At the Swedish Post and Telecom Authority (PTS), several internal professional networks provide the opportunity for staff members from different departments and units to come together and discuss topics of mutual interest. The structure and set-up of the networks differ depending on the theme and purpose and may shift over time. Topics include workshop facilitation, competitive intelligence or simply providing a forum for all the lawyers in the authority to meet and discuss.

One of the more long-standing and established networks is themed around supervision. PTS is organised so that supervision of market actors takes place in different departments and based on different legislation and regulations. The Supervision forum is a chance for all staff members actively working on supervision to exchange views and ideas but also a way for PTS to try to ensure coherence in its processes across departments. Although the supervision is based to some extent on different legal frameworks, and there may be justified reasons for different approaches, the aim is to have coherent processes when possible.

The forum meets twice a year and in between there are possibilities for exchange of information on ongoing cases or other interesting topics. Often there are external speakers invited as well, providing perspectives on supervision from other regulators or, for example, the Parliamentary Ombudsmen, that responsible for ensuring that public authorities and their staff comply with the laws and other statues governing their actions. The forum is administrated by a group of staff members working on supervision in different departments.

Source: Information provided by ACCC/AER 2020 (updated in 2021) and PTS, 2020.

---

## Process

### *Governing body and decision making*

**A number of safeguards are in place to ensure adequate qualifications and integrity of board members, but a new legislative proposal could dilute the independent nature of regulatory decision-making.** Board members are currently selected by a committee comprising the PCM and ministries, and the terms of board members are staggered. Candidates are required to have adequate professional and academic qualifications, and for the executive president there is a requirement to sit a public exam that tests candidates' sectoral expertise. However, a legislative proposal introduced to the Congressional Commission in September 2021, Law Proposal 21/2021-CR, proposes to add representatives of user and consumer associations and non-governmental organisations to the board. These representatives would not be subject to the same requirements for professional and academic experience. The proposal risks confusing the role of the board of economic regulators with stakeholder engagement fora. Assigning stakeholder representatives to the Sunass board would weaken the basis for impartial, predictable and expert regulatory decision-making.

**The part-time nature of board positions may leave little time for strategic decision-making.** The board of Sunass has a wide mandate, with exclusive responsibility for regulatory decision making (except for sanctioning decisions) as well as for setting the strategic direction of the organisation and monitoring performance. Board members operate on a part-time basis, meeting twice a month, and tend to have other occupations as well. Extraordinary board meetings take place when necessary, but are not remunerated. The part-time nature of board positions can result in an uneven balance between the time dedicated to regulatory decision-making and strategic discussion. In practice, board members rarely reject regulatory proposals, although they may ask to expand on reports or make additional considerations. In addition, lengthy selection procedures can sometimes result in vacant board seats, further reducing the level of scrutiny the board can exert.

**Given the limited time that the board can dedicate to preparatory work, the general management and so-called "pre-board meetings" play an essential role to safeguard the quality of regulatory decision making.** In practice, the General Management of Sunass acts as a hub through which all proposals pass, after which the proposals are presented to the Executive President and the board. It also provides a platform for cross-organisational alignment, where input from other directorates can be sought during the pre-board meetings. In a context where board members only have limited time to prepare for board meetings, the pre-board meetings can serve as a useful tool to increase scrutiny of regulatory decision making.

### *Recommendations*

Short term:

- **Ensure** sufficient time and resources to board members for strategic decision making (Box 1.8). Such matters could include, for example, prioritisation of those activities that contribute most towards the regulator's strategic objectives in a context of scarce resources.
- **Assess** possibilities to delegate certain decision-making responsibilities to the technical body of the regulator, to provide more focus in the board's responsibilities towards strategic decision-making. Any delegation of decision-making should be accompanied by appropriate transparency and accountability mechanisms to hold decision makers at all levels of the organisation to account.
- **Retain** and defend the requirement that all board members should have adequate professional and academic qualifications and be subject to identical vetting requirements. Sunass may also seek ways to strengthen and institutionalise stakeholder engagement but firmly outside of the board of the regulator (see Engagement and transparency of engagement process).

Medium term:

- **Continue** the good practice of public exams for the executive president and consider introducing this requirement for all board members. This could provide stronger safeguards to ensure the right level of qualifications for all board members.
- **Strengthen** the overall level of board engagement. In this effort, Sunass could consider:
  - Advocating for a legislative change allowing full-time board positions;
  - Organising more frequent board meetings; or
  - Providing remuneration to board members for extraordinary board meetings.

---

### Box 1.8. Governing Board of Mexico's Federal Telecommunications Institute (IFT)

The 2013 reform of the Mexican constitution established the IFT as an autonomous, independent public agency with its own decision-making power and operations, with legal personality and its own assets. The authority was created for regulating spectrum, networks, services, competition and efficient development of the broadcasting and telecommunications sectors. It also acts as competition authority for these markets.

The Governing Board is the Institute's highest instance of governance and decision making. It is composed of seven full-time Commissioners with voting rights, including its president. The IFT Chair presides the Governing Board and Institute, and is its legal representative.

---

> The Commissioners remain in office for nine years. Their mandates are staggered to allow for continuity and are non-renewable. All commissioners have one vote, weigh in on complex decision-making in the sector and have non-delegable duties. All the Commissioners have to attend plenary sessions except for justifiable cause. Their powers are not limited and they are on an equal footing.
>
> Source: information provided by IFT, 2018.

### Regulatory quality tools

**Sunass's current use of regulatory impact assessment (RIA) shows some deficiencies, but the regulator is already making strides to improve practices.** The 2016 OECD report *Regulatory Policy in Peru* identified a lack of *ex ante* impact assessment across regulators in Peru (OECD, 2016[7]). There is only a limited approach towards cost-benefit analysis, which means not all costs are measured, making it difficult to compare different regulatory options. Moreover, there is no proportionality requirement to tailor the level of assessment to the potential impacts of new regulations. To improve practices and align with international best practice, Sunass received technical assistance from the OECD and internal guidelines for regulatory impact assessment were developed in 2021 (OECD, 2021[8]).

**Sunass does not conduct *ex post* evaluation of regulations, missing a chance to assess their effectiveness and highlight the organisation's impact in the sector.** *Ex post* evaluation of regulations is a useful tool to analyse if intended goals have been achieved and whether approaches need to be adjusted. Especially in a context with more complex changes to the regulatory framework (such as the new responsibilities of Sunass in rural areas and its efforts towards the integration of service providers), *ex post* evaluation can improve insights on the regulator's effectiveness.

*Recommendations*

Short term:

- **Implement** the technical guidelines on RIA approved in 2021, as part of the reforms following the OECD's technical assistance.
- **Assign** the quality control for RIA to another body outside the Directorate of Policies and Regulations, to ensure a minimum level of quality for all RIA.

Medium term:

- **Establish** RIA as a mandatory step in the development of all regulations, with only limited exceptions based on clear criteria.
- **Use** the reform and approval of the internal RIA guidelines to make RIA operational across the whole organisation. In this effort, Sunass should:
  - Ensure swift implementation and awareness across the organisation for the RIA guidelines, in order to establish clear processes, criteria for exceptions and procedures for public consultation.
  - Target the use of RIA in proportion to the significance of the regulation. The depth of the RIA should depend on the size of the regulatory impact, focusing efforts on the most important and impactful regulatory measures (OECD, 2020[9]).
  - Compare alternative options based on wider costs and benefits. The wider costs include "direct costs (administrative, financial and capital costs) as well as indirect costs (opportunity costs) whether borne by businesses, citizens or government" (OECD, 2012[10]).

- **Introduce** systematic *ex post* evaluation of all (significant) regulations, a necessary condition to ensure that regulations are effective and efficient (OECD, 2012[10]). In doing so, Sunass should take into account the recommendations made in the 2020 OECD report *Reviewing the Stock of Regulation*. These recommend among others to safeguard that "*ex post* reviews should be an integral and permanent part of the regulatory cycle" and "consultations need to be undertaken with affected parties, using processes that are as accessible as possible". *Ex post* evaluations should be implemented progressively, starting with pilot projects but moving towards systematic application across the organisation.

### Regulatory enforcement and inspections

**Sunass has a limited range of sanctions to effectively tackle poor performance by EPs, and many EPs enter a "transitional regime" that impacts the continuity of the sector.** Sunass reports that monetary sanctions have had limited success in reducing the high levels of non-compliance in the sector. The regulator also has the ability to remove the management of EPs, but this mechanism focuses on cases where management does not meet the legal requirements needed to hold the position or in case of conflict of interest. A limited enforcement toolkit to incentivise better performance of EPs, combined with other sectoral challenges such as financial constraints, means currently 19 out of 50 EPs have entered into the Transitional Support Regime (RAT) on grounds of poor performance. These companies are run by OTASS for a maximum period of 15 years. The success of this regime will depend on the ability to establish an improvement in the management beyond the short-term, to ensure sustainability of the sector.

**Sunass's use of a differentiated approach to enforcement for rural providers seems reasonable and pragmatic, but it is not yet clear if approaches are leading to the desired behavioural change and compliance.** Although within its powers, Sunass has decided not to sanction rural providers for a period of at least two years, in contrast to its approach to enforcement for EPs. Sunass instead provides support and incentives for rural providers to improve service provision. Given the relatively short time that this approach has been in place, there is no evidence yet on whether this differentiation is resulting in the desired outcomes.

**Sector supervision is challenging due to the large number and different types of providers, Sunass's limited capacity for inspections and a lack of compliance culture.** The decentralised offices only have a limited reach due to their capacity, which makes it especially difficult to reach out to all 50 EPs and 25 000 rural service providers. A report by OCI also highlights the limited capacity of Sunass's Supervision Directorate, and Sunass reports that its lack of financial resources results in underfinanced supervision activities. Sunass relies on a strategy to involve the ATMs in the engagement with rural providers. The ATMs perform a crucial role with the potential to increase the regulator's reach towards all rural providers. However, the capacities of ATMs also tend to be limited. This results in a low overall capacity for inspections of the different types of providers. Moreover, 70% of the corrective measures identified through inspections of EPs in 2020 were not implemented, leading to sanctioning actions. Breaches are frequently linked to non-compliance in terms of control of treatment processes, operational aspects and quality of billing. Given the low overall compliance and complex sector context, Sunass has implemented a number of compliance promotion activities, such as benchmarking, guidance sessions on regulations and workshops on good corporate governance. This effort to build capacities, which can support a culture of compliance and performance, is made more difficult by the high level of turnover of both leadership and staff in water utilities. Furthermore, the political appointment of utility managers limits both operational effectiveness and long term planning.

**Many other supervisory bodies have responsibilities in the sector, but low levels of collaboration create inefficiencies.** These findings show similarities with findings in the 2020 OECD report on the Environmental Evaluation and Enforcement Agency of Peru (*Organismo de Evaluación y Fiscalización Ambiental* – OEFA), which noted in that context a need for a greater level of co-ordination, more clarity on mandates and improvements in data sharing among institutions (OECD, 2020[11]). In the water sector, different bodies supervise and enforce aspects of service delivery that are in many cases closely related or even dependent on each other. For example, the supervision on the frequency of quality testing is performed by the Health Authority in case the EP has a quality control plan, but is done by Sunass in case there is no such plan (which in practice is often the case). There are currently no joined-up approaches to overall inspections and the level of interaction and sharing of data remains low. This can lead to information asymmetries that could harm the effectiveness of supervision and enforcement.

### *Recommendations*

Short term:

- **Increase** the interaction with other supervisory bodies in the sector, analysing potential benefits of joined-up approaches to inspections and institutionalisation of information sharing, enhancing the effectiveness and efficiency of the overall framework.

- **Make** the outcomes of inspections publicly available in cases where this is legally possible, to increase citizen awareness and improve transparency.

Medium term:

- **Incentivise** a behavioural change towards compliance and an improvement of outcomes. In this effort, Sunass could:
  - ○ Make use of behaviourally informed approaches towards compliance and performance, especially in those areas where the more traditional means of enforcement are either unavailable or not effective. In these efforts, transparency on the performance of utilities through tailored communication could support public scrutiny. Sunass could make use of the guidance included in the *OECD Regulatory Enforcement and Inspections Toolkit* on the use of compliance promotion and risk-based approaches as part of the regulatory toolkit (OECD, 2018[12]).
  - ○ Experiment with more risk-based approaches towards inspections, and a shift in focus from procedural compliance towards outcomes. This is particularly important in a context where hands-on supervision of all providers may be impracticable, and in light of overall low levels of compliance. Risk-based and outcome-focused approaches could direct the regulator's actions towards the most troublesome areas of performance and focus on those violations that matter most, to have the biggest impact (Box 1.9; Box 1.10; Box 1.11).
  - ○ Continue the good practice of providing guidance rather than sanctioning rural providers. Sunass should carefully consider alternative strategies for rural providers to incentivise compliance, such as benchmarking and publicising of good practices, based on the available evidence and responsive to the profile of providers. This could be done through a mapping of the origins of non-compliance and the potential intervention points at which the regulator could influence practice, to analyse the effectiveness of different options (*causal pathway methodology*).

---

**Box 1.9. Verified trust and accountability (VTA) regulatory approach for small-scale and off-grid water, sewerage and energy services used by the Essential Services Commission of South Australia (ESCOSA)**

ESCOSA is adopting a verified trust and accountability (VTA) regulatory approach to the way it regulates small-scale and off-grid water, sewerage and energy services in South Australia. The VTA approach provides a targeted, flexible approach to regulation. This is to ensure that the regulatory

---

frameworks it applies under industry regulation Acts is consistent with its primary statutory objective, and is proportionate and responsive to recent and emerging issues. Those issues can relate to changing technological, operational, environmental or other factors impacting the delivery of water and sewerage retail services, and the sale and/or supply of electricity and gas services to South Australians through small-scale networks.

As well as accounting for existing compliance obligations, the new approach is designed to place more transparency and emphasis on licensed small-scale networks providing assurance to their customers and the Commission, that the services they provide are sustainable over the medium to longer term.

The approach will formally begin in July 2022 after an implementation phase, during which the Commission will work with licensees to produce baseline data sets with which the Commission will categorise each licensee. The categorisation of licensees forms part of introducing the VTA approach. The Commission will assess each licensee on compliance and sustainability performance and place it in one of two categories:

- Category A: Licensees considered trusted to competently run their networks with less prescriptive regulatory oversight. Category A licensees benefit from reduced regulatory reporting.
- Category B: Licensees where there are concerns regarding network performance, with respect to either compliance, medium to long-term service sustainability, or both – and there does not appear to be a credible, measurable remediation strategy. This does not imply or mean that the licensee's operation is unsafe but indicates that customers are facing a higher level of service risk than appropriate.

A fact sheet outlines the methodology used to categorise licensees.

The Commission will work with and monitor Category B licensees as they develop and implement remediation strategies, with the goal of future reassessment as Category A. The results of the assessment for each licensed operator will be publicly available. This ensures customers and licensees have transparency regarding the outcome of the assessment.

Source: https://www.escosa.sa.gov.au/projects-and-publications/projects/corporate/verified-trust-accountability-regulatory-approach-to-small-scale-networks; ESCOSA (2021), Final Inquiry Report : Inquiry into regulatory arrangements for small-scale water, sewerage and energy services, https://www.escosa.sa.gov.au/articledocuments/1005/20210713-inquiry-smallscalenetwork-finalreport.pdf.aspx?embed=y.

---

## Box 1.10. Risk-based approach to inspections in Greece

Since 2016, Greece, under the initiative of the General Secretariat for Industry within the Ministry of Development and Investment, is conducting a holistic effort to transform the business environment. This effort includes a simplification of licensing procedures and a transition of inspection systems to a risk-based approach.

Law 4512/2018 introduced for the first time the principles of risk-based supervision, which aims to improve consumer welfare by reducing risks (existing or potential) to the public interest, such as health, safety and environmental protection. At the same time, it aims to create the environment for an effective and efficient inspections mechanism without additional (or unnecessary) burden to businesses.

The new framework focuses on the compliance of businesses, through the introduction of innovative tools, such as checklists for inspections, risk-based planning, a complaint management system (CMS) and the Enforcement Management Model (EMM). The Greek inspection system consists of three steps: 1) planning 2) execution and 3) compliance.

1. Planning: Planning of inspections is conducted on an annual basis and risk criteria are determined by the competent authorities. The main criteria are: a) the evaluation of the risk an economic activity poses to public interest, b) the available resources of the authority and c) the results of previous inspections.

2. Execution: Inspections of economic activities are conducted through checklists. A checklist contains both questions to collect information on the business and questions that facilitate the inspector to examine the compliance of the business with the applicable legislation. It is an evaluation tool containing the essential requirements or categories of requirements directly related to the potential risk of the specific activity and with which businesses must comply. Carrying out inspections through these checklists ensures effective decision-making on addressing identified risks.

3. Compliance and EMM: Aiming to ensure compliance of economic activities based on proportionate criteria (also risk-based), Greece has developed the Enforcement Management Model (EMM). The EMM is a "decision tree", which provides inspectors with the appropriate guidance, criteria and parameters before deciding on the appropriate measures, if violations are identified.

The important element of the EMM is to "drive" inspectors not to impose fines or other strict administrative measures, if compliance can be achieved through softer measures, such as guidance to the business or written recommendations, measures that also build trust between the public and the private sector. The decision is based on risk analysis, as well as the principles of proportionality, transparency and uniformity. In the nexus of this system is not the imposition of a fine or of a stricter measure, but the support of businesses to comply with regulations, as compliance is a prerequisite for a friendly and competitive business environment. Thus, the first available tool for the inspector is the provision of guidance and consulting (Table 1.4).

### Table 1.4. Measures based on risk categorisation

| Level of Compliance | Types of measures of compliance | | | | | | |
|---|---|---|---|---|---|---|---|
| | Guidance and consulting | Written recommendation for compliance | Imposition of fine | Temporary or permanent closure | Ban of products | Report to public prosecutor's offices | Administrative sanctions based on legislation |
| High-risk (important violation) | ✓ | ✓ | ✓ | ✓ | ✓ | ✓ | ✓ |
| Medium risk (moderate infringement) | ✓ | ✓ | ✓ | - | - | - | ✓ |
| Low risk (minor infringement) | ✓ | ✓ | - | - | - | - | - |

Greece will undergo an evaluation of the supervision tools in the next years, however, so far the system shows positive results and supports the efforts for a better regulatory environment for businesses in Greece. In addition, it provides a system that is transparent and fair by shifting the paradigm, as public authorities do not follow the punitive-oriented inspections system but encourage and support businesses to achieve the necessary compliance. Therefore, a relationship of trust and co-operation is built between the government and businesses.

Source: Information provided by the Secretary General for Industry in Greece, 2021.

## Box 1.11. The ACCC's compliance and enforcement strategy

In Australia, the Australian Competition & Consumer Commission (ACCC) has developed a compliance and enforcement strategy that is communicated to all stakeholders. The agency uses four integrated strategies to achieve the compliance objectives:

- Encouraging compliance with the law by educating and informing consumers and businesses about their rights and responsibilities.
- Enforcing the law, including resolution of possible contraventions both administratively and by litigation and other formal enforcement outcomes.
- Undertaking market studies or reporting on emerging competition or consumer issues with a view to identifying any market failures and how to address them, and to support and inform the compliance and enforcement measures and identify possible areas for policy consideration.
- Working with other agencies to implement these strategies, including through co-ordinated approaches.

The ACCC is selective in the matters to investigate and the sectors in which the agency engages in education and market analysis. The ACCC uses annual compliance and enforcement priorities to inform decision making in this regard.

In deciding which compliance or enforcement tool (or the combination of such tools) to use, the first priority is always to achieve the best possible outcome for the community and to manage risk proportionately. The ACCC's enforcement actions seek to maximise impact across an industry sector. For example, the agency uses the outcome of one court proceeding to encourage other industry participants in the sector to improve their practices.

The ACCC's role is to focus on those circumstances that will, or have the potential to, harm the competitive process or result in widespread consumer detriment. The ACCC therefore exercises discretion to direct resources to matters that provide the greatest overall benefit.

Each year the ACCC reviews the compliance and enforcement priorities. Priorities are determined following external consultation and an assessment of existing or emerging issues and their impact on the regulated matters. The ACCC publicly announces its priorities in February each year. The priorities are released with the aim of promoting market wide compliance with the law and to manage public expectations regarding the ACCC's ability to take on additional matters outside its priority areas. A number of key stakeholders in Australia actively respond to the ACCC's announcement of the priorities and take active measures to improve compliance.

Source: Information provided by ACCC, 2021.

### Engagement and transparency of engagement process

**The Users Councils have the potential to increase the engagement of users in the regulatory process, but would have to be strengthened to fulfil this ambition.** Activity levels differ across councils, where only the Lima User Council meets on a regular basis. While the councils are intended to be composed of five to six members, in practice this is not the case. In addition, Users Councils should have representation of unserved or underserved groups, which in practice does not appear to be the case, representing a lost opportunity to capture different perspectives in user priorities. Users Councils rarely submit opinions, or carry out events on regulatory issues or transmit user queries with communities, which are part of their functions. Moreover, they do not receive any resources from Sunass. All Peruvian economic regulators are required to establish Users Councils and there are significant differences between sectors in how they function and provide their inputs. There would be scope for cross-learning between regulators to increase the added value of this engagement mechanism.

**Sunass faces the challenge to engage all consumers in the regulatory process, including the hard-to-reach and potential consumers.** Sunass's engagement with users is centred on complaints and disputes but input into regulatory decision-making is relatively limited. As both the scope of public consultation and the involvement of Users Councils are limited, Sunass may not be able to engage with all consumers, to ensure their perspectives and interests are sufficiently considered in regulatory decision-making. As only 13% of consumers are aware of Sunass's functions and many materials are not available in local languages, many vulnerable consumers will be unaware of the possibility to engage in the regulatory process to provide input and submit opinions. This may be the case especially for consumers in rural areas or those without internet access. However, engagement with all types of current and potential consumers will be crucial in a context of resistance towards paying a tariff for water.

**Beyond Users Councils, Peru's economic regulators are not required to establish other stakeholder engagement bodies, and Sunass could learn from the experience of other countries to strengthen practice.** Draft regulations are open to public comment, but Sunass does not always hold a public hearing to collect input from stakeholders. The 2021 report *Implementing Regulatory Impact Assessment at Peru's National Superintendence of Sanitation Services* assesses that Sunass currently does not have a mechanism for early consultation of regulatory proposals, which could result in a lack of information and input to identify policy issues (OECD, 2021[8]). There may be scope, in particular in the water and sanitation sector, where compliance and capacity are an issue, to enhance the involvement of operators in the regulatory process using fora bringing together all relevant stakeholders and experts.

*Recommendations*

Short term:

- **Ensure** public hearings are conducted on all new regulatory proposals with a relevant impact on stakeholders.
- **Establish** more frequent meetings between Sunass and the Users Councils, allowing an on-going discussion on upcoming regulatory proposals, wider sector challenges and the role of the regulator within the sector.
- **Provide** an increased level of transparency on input by Users Councils, by publishing opinions on regulatory proposals and a response from the regulator on Sunass's website.
- **Strengthen** the inputs of Users Councils into the decision-making process. To empower the councils, Sunass could consider:
  - Ensuring that Users Council membership is representative of the diversity of users in Peru;
  - The allocation of a minimum level of resources that could facilitate the participation of Users Councils;
  - The provision of training to members of Users Councils to explain the regulatory framework and discuss ways in which they can contribute towards the regulatory decision making; and
  - Periodic exchanges between Peruvian economic regulators on the experiences and good practices regarding engaging Users Councils in the regulatory process, to create mutual learning opportunities.
- **Consider** alternative mechanisms to improve the level of interaction with vulnerable consumers, including more targeted communication in plain language and local languages.

Medium term:

- **Increase** the added-value and impact of stakeholder engagement, to go beyond a mere legislative requirement and establish it as a main element within the regulatory decision-making process (Box 1.12). In this effort, Sunass could consider:

  - Using early consultation as a tool to engage with all stakeholders and collect input that feeds into the analysis of the complexity of the issue and the appropriateness of potential regulatory options; and

  - Exploring the creation of ad-hoc or permanent stakeholder engagement bodies that would bring together all stakeholders, and possibly sector experts, to provide early inputs to the regulatory process and to seek to create exchange of views on plans and challenges (Box 1.13).

---

**Box 1.12. Engagement, consultation and transparency practices at Portugal's Energy Services Regulatory Authority (ERSE)**

ERSE's decision-making processes include a series of mechanisms to promote stakeholder engagement, consultation and transparency. These include the use of:

- Public consultations
- Stakeholder consultations
- Pre-consultations
- Public hearings
- Consultative councils

The ERSE Statutes require the regulator to consult all interested parties and the general public before approving or amending any regulation. Such a consultation must foresee a period of 30 working days for the submission of comments and suggestion. The submissions received are made public, unless the author has explicitly requested confidentiality. Furthermore, ERSE is required to substantiate its decisions in writing, including in relation to the criticisms or suggestions that may have been made to its draft decision.

In addition, ERSE may hold tailored stakeholder consultations, where a regulatory decision affects a specific group of stakeholders. For exceptional and urgent situations, the statutes also allow ERSE to undertake a rapid consultation, of minimum eight consecutive days, addressed to directly affected stakeholders. For particularly complex or sensitive issues, ERSE may also conduct pre-consultations before the presentation of a regulatory proposal in order to identify stakeholders' main concerns. This preliminary step does not substitute the obligation for full consultation.

Internal procedures for the various types of consultations ensure that the consultation process is conducted in a consistent and reliable manner across all departments and policy areas. These practical guidelines include among other things: standardised templates and required supporting and explanatory documents; the information to be provided via the publication page on the website; the correct calculation for the consultation period; the handling of confidential information and personal data; as well as a step-by-step guide on the consultation launch, closure, evaluation and finalisation of the regulatory decision. As part of the consultation, ERSE publishes its proposals, supporting analysis and parameters, cost-benefit studies and other inputs which substantiate its draft decision.

In addition to the written consultation process, ERSE systematically holds public hearings when developing regulatory measures. Traditionally hosted as face-to-face meetings, ERSE has increasingly employed digital technologies to broaden its outreach and ensure that its engagement efforts are not diminished due to epidemiological or other crises.

---

ERSE also consults key stakeholders on its various decisions through three independent advisory bodies that deliver non-binding opinions (see Box 1.13 for more details).

ERSE combines rigorous consultation processes with quicker processes in urgent and extraordinary cases, allowing for nimble decision-making when required, as well as extensive communication and publication practices. As of October 2021, ERSE had concluded a total of 100 public consultations since its creation. On average, consultations have lasted 144 days (5 months); in two cases, the process took two years to complete.

Source: Information provided by ERSE, 2021.

## Box 1.13. The role of consultative bodies in the regulatory decision-making process at Portugal's Energy Services Regulatory Authority (ERSE)

ERSE's Statutes form the foundation for the regulator's inclusive and transparent decision-making approach, through the creation of three consultative bodies (known as councils), which contribute to the development of its technical regulations, tariff decisions and the broad lines of action and deliberations taken by ERSE's Board of Directors. The three consultative councils – Advisory Council, Tariff Council and Fuels Council – act as a forum for creating consensus among key stakeholders.

As part of a broader consultation and engagement policy (see Box 1.12), the councils issue non-binding opinions on ERSE's regulatory proposals. Importantly, where the regulator does not take on board the opinions presented by the councils, it must justify in writing why it has not adopted the council's proposed changes. Together with ERSE's other engagement mechanisms, this process ensures accountability and strengthens the integrity of the regulator's decisions. In addition, they provide a permanent platform for stakeholders to meet and understand each other's perspectives. In this way, the councils provide stability to stakeholders and achieve consensus in their statements in an impressive 90% of cases.

The councils are composed of a broad spectrum of representation from national, regional and municipal government, consumer organisations and the energy industry. Council members serve a non-remunerated and renewable term of three years. Each council decides how often to meet in order to prepare its opinions. Generally speaking, and in response to the increased activities and responsibilities of the regulator, the councils may meet several times a month. All opinions of the councils are approved by majority vote, although if members do not agree with all or parts of the opinion of the council they can state this in the submission to ERSE. The opinions of the councils are made public and published on the ERSE website.

Given the characteristic asymmetry of information and resources between the industry and consumers, ERSE seeks to facilitate the latter's engagement in a number of ways. First, industry and consumer representatives must be represented in equal numbers. Second, ERSE provides a subsistence and attendance allowance for consumer representatives, as well as for government, public bodies and representatives from Azores and Madeira. In addition, ERSE provides training to the household consumer associations that sit on its consultative councils in order to build their capacity and ability to contribute to deliberations.

Source: Information provided by ERSE, 2021.

*Complaints*

**Challenges in the sector are exemplified by the high number of complaints Sunass receives; greater value could be extracted from this information if it was analysed in a systematic way.** Although Sunass is only the third recourse for consumer complaints, the regulator receives a high volume of complaints, indicating that the direct mechanism to file complaints first with providers is not successful in settling differences. In an attempt to resolve problems before an official complaint is pursued, Sunass launched the 'Participa vecino' initiative to create a platform for more informal exchange between users and service providers, using micro-hearings to address disputes and answer questions. Through its complaints function, Sunass collects useful information on current issues in the sector, which could be used to inform other functions such as supervision or the drafting of regulation. Insights from complaints are sometimes used to inform other areas of Sunass's functions, but this is not done systematically.

*Recommendations*

Short term:

- **Assess** how to improve communication towards consumers around tariff increases, the overall functioning of the sector and the rationale for paying for water services, and understanding their bills, to make sure consumers understand their rights in these situations and what can be expected from Sunass. As part of this effort, Sunass could consider using behavioural insights to increase the willingness of consumers to pay a tariff for drinking water and sanitation services.

Medium term:

- **Use** the insights from the complaints procedure to feed into other processes to improve Sunass's actions and sector performance. Sunass could conduct an analysis on the topics of consumer complaints, and publish the resulting report, to increase insights. These insights can be used to:
  - Strengthen the effectiveness of regulatory processes, by aiming the actions at the most problematic areas and subsequently decreasing the number of complaints;
  - Provide targeted training and/or guidelines to EPs, to enable them to provide clear information on user rights and the responsibilities of providers related to the most frequent areas of complaints (such as was done in the case of complaints related to tariff increases). This could bring as a result that more complaints are dealt with in a satisfactory manner between users and providers, supporting the effectiveness of the mechanism to file complaints with providers first.

## Output and outcome

### Data collection, analysis and management

**Sunass, alongside other public bodies in the sector, is confronted with poor availability of data on sector performance, and has employed a number of initiatives to address this shortcoming.** Since 2004, Sunass has collected data from the EPs that is defined in regulation. However, in practice, the regulation is not reviewed often enough to remain aligned with data needs, causing a discrepancy with actual data collection practices. Through its decentralised offices and ATMs, Sunass has also collected data on 2 000 out of 25 000 rural providers – a big improvement given the initial lack of data. On the other hand, the regulator is still far away from achieving a universal data coverage for the entire sector.

**Sunass's efforts to improve efficiency and drive sector transformation are made more difficult due to a lack of reliable and consistent data.** Data is the bedrock of evidence-based economic regulation, but many factors affect the quality of the data Sunass has at its disposal. Data quality tends to be low due to inconsistency in data management practices and low capacity of staff in utilities. Sunass faces challenges to train staff in providers given their high turnover rate. Finally, a lack of automation and IT infrastructure due to budget constraints, as well as difficult formats in which data is sometimes submitted, can make data validation processes long and internal data sharing and usage more difficult.

**The relatively low level of data sharing between public institutions in the sector undermines an efficient use of resources and could pose an additional burden on regulated entities.** Data sharing is not institutionalised, but rather depends on personal interactions and relationships. MVCS leads the management and integration of information systems on the sector, but interoperability with Sunass's system is not yet effective. There are a number of efforts to improve data sharing but progress is slow. A low level of data sharing means that providers are sometimes required to report the same data to different institutions, through different systems.

*Recommendations*

Short term:

- **Assess** whether current requirements in terms of data reliability (most notably, the sworn statement) are sufficient to guarantee data quality, and in which cases additional requirements such as an audit may be preferable and possible.
- **Promote** data sharing and collective data collection through the establishment of institutional data agreements with other public bodies such as OTASS, MVCS and the National Statistics Institute (INEI) (Box 1.14).

Medium term:

- **Earmark** the implementation of IT strategies, such as automation, digitalisation and the move to cloud-based systems, as a priority within the budgetary planning process. Improvements in data usage and sharing within the institution have the potential to increase the efficiency of operations as well as the effectiveness of actions, and should therefore receive priority.
- **Assess** whether all the data collected from utilities is necessary and used by the regulator, and update the regulation on data collection if needed. Data requirements should be clearly understood and not too onerous for firms.
- **Provide** online training and guidance documents to EPs on data definitions and ways to record and submit data. This could support a more standardised method of data collection, based on easy-to-process data formats. To account for high levels of staff turnover in EPs, these trainings and documents should be delivered in a format that can be accessed at any time.
- **Build** upon Sunass's rural data collection efforts so far, to expand the data availability and include a larger share of the communal organisations. To achieve this, Sunass could further empower ATMs and assess the potential for automation and digitalisation in the data collection processes.

---

**Box 1.14. Sharing and using data to better manage risks in Italy**

A number of Italian regions and institutions have, in recent years, worked on improving data sharing, analysis and usage, to reduce the burdens and inefficiencies created by duplications and lack of coordination between different services, and better support regional economies.

In Lombardy, the Mo.Ri.Ca system for risk monitoring in construction sites uses data emerging from notifications, surveillance and accidents (collected via Impres@BI) and estimates the risk level of a given site on this basis. Risk criteria and weights, previously defined empirically, are now being improved through Machine Learning. The key strength of the system is that it integrates data from a

---

number of sources, including notifications from the health care system, and considerably improves risk management at a very limited cost.

In Campania, in addition to the existing GISA system to plan and manage all food safety inspections, the region partnered with the University of Naples Parthenope to develop MytiluSE, a system to predict the quality of waters so as to secure safety of mussels produced in the bay of Naples. Rather than expending large resources on *ex post* controls to find potential contamination, the system works preemptively, enabling to know which days the harvesting of mussels would be unsafe. Once fully operational, it can both inform producers and guide inspectors' work. Developing the system involved investigating the currents of the bay of Naples, mapping contamination sources, and developing a reliable predictive model, but it is potentially completely transformative for regulatory delivery. It was also adapted to predict air pollution by fumes, which can affect feed for bovine herds. The predictive approach for mussels is not only better for the economy and public service efficiency, but it also avoids health hazards far more effectively, because microbiological testing and sampling takes time, and results can come too late (leading to potential contaminations from other products harvested the same day).

Source: Montella R, Riccio A, di Luccio D, Mellone G, de Vita, C G (2020), MytiluSE: Modelling mytilus farming System with Enhanced web technologies, Università degli Studi di Napoli Parthenope, Sciences and Technology Dipartiment, commissioned by Campania Region, Unità Operativa Dirigenziale Prevenzione e Sanità Pubblica Veterinaria (presentation), as cited in (OECD, 2021[13]), OECD Regulatory Policy Outlook 2021, OECD Publishing, Paris, https://doi.org/10.1787/38b0fdb1-en.

### Monitoring and reporting on the performance of the sector

**Sunass's benchmarking creates a powerful tool to incentivise sector performance, and could be further improved to hold operators to account.** Benchmarking providers gives behavioural incentives to improve performance, through the *naming and shaming* of good and poor performance. This approach to performance reporting may be especially important in a context with many publicly owned providers. However, data is not presented in a way that allows the public to use the findings to hold operators to account. Sunass does not publish trends over time for individual key performance indicators, but instead focuses its reporting on a composite indicator on the performance of operators. This more aggregated reporting weakens the incentives that result from the benchmark.

*Recommendations*

Short term:

- **Enable** tracking of utility performance through wider public access to disaggregated data underlying indicators and historical trends. Emphasis should be on the importance to provide straightforward data and indicators that stakeholders can interpret without trouble, as well as easy-to-read charts on changes in performance over time (Box 1.15).

Medium term:

- **Consult** with stakeholders on the data needs and insights they are most interested in, and conduct regular checks to ensure data remains accessible.

## Box 1.15. Sector data transparency initiatives by regulators

### Sector data transparency initiative by Mexico's Federal Telecommunications Institute (IFT)

The Telecommunications Information Bank (Banco de Información de Telecomunicaciones, BIT) is an interactive tool for consulting, analysing, exploring and downloading data on the telecommunications sector. The portal is equipped with data exploration modules, in which users can download disaggregated information and historical series in open data format.

The BIT is a portal that incorporates good practices in terms of open data and access to information. The IFT made the BIT platform available to the public in order to disseminate and promote the use of information on the regulated sector that IFT uses to monitor and regulate the telecommunications and broadcasting sectors in Mexico. The BIT contributes to: i) generating knowledge on the performance of telecommunications and broadcasting in Mexico; ii) strengthening the decision making of the different public and private actors involved in these sectors and, iii) strengthening the design of public policies.

The BIT enables users to consult information regarding the macroeconomic environment of telecommunications and broadcasting in Mexico, revenues and investment of operators, as well as indicators related to the different services such as fixed and mobile telephony, fixed and mobile broadband and television. It also has a data download module and a graphic explorer to perform customised queries, generate variables, perform complex sectoral analyses, build indicator dashboards and graphically analyse time series.

The BIT is a dynamic information platform that is expected to evolve over time. In the medium term, the published tables will be updated every quarter, in addition to validating historical information for long-term analysis. Further improvements could include the addition of information not published to date, such as marketing and bundling metrics, in order to monitor the convergence of telecommunications services.

### Open Data at the Swedish Energy Markets Inspectorate

Open data at the Swedish Energy Market Inspectorate (Ei) are information available for anyone to use, re-use and share, so others can develop it and create benefits for more people. The information is made available without restriction in the form of copyright, patents or confidentiality, by being free of personal data and otherwise confidential information.

Ei works actively with open data in accordance with directives and recommendations from the European Union (EU) and the government. The re-use of government information is regulated by the PSI Act (PSI stands for Public Sector Information, i.e. public information). The law is based on the EU PSI Directive.

Ei's data sources are catalogued according to international standards in a directory service that, in addition to the reference/access point/API to the data itself, contains metadata description of the data sources according to the DCAT-AP standard. The catalogue is "harvested", i.e. loaded and published on the national catalogue of open data (http://www.dataportal.se) and the EU open data catalogue (http://www.europeandataportal.eu).

The data catalogue lists all of Ei's open data and Ei's statistics portal contains the datasets published as statistics. Ei is continuously working to make more data available and will increase the range in the data catalogue. Currently the data catalogue includes open data on, for example, outage indicators, network tariffs and prices, customers per type of subscription, companies' income statements and balance sheets, and technical data related to the electricity network (https://www.ei.se/om-webbplatsen/psi/).

### Monitoring and reporting on the performance of Sunass

**In line with good practice, Sunass's strategic objectives are monitored and reported on through indicators with time-bound targets.** Sunass uses a compact set of eight indicators linked to specific strategic objectives, which it reports on through its annual report (Table 1.5). It also connects the data on indicators with financial information, to give insights into the regulator's effectiveness in its use of resources. Furthermore, performance reporting on indicators is complemented with other data on performance in terms of efficiency, number of tariff studies, reports and compliance, which provide further insights on Sunass's performance. Though not a legal requirement, Sunass shows good practice by sharing its annual report and performance report with Congress, strengthening the accountability of the regulator.

### Table 1.5. Indicators and goals linked to Sunass's strategic objectives

Sunass strategic plan (PEI) 2020-24

| Objective (OEI) | Indicator | Goals | | | | |
|---|---|---|---|---|---|---|
| | | 2020 | 2021 | 2022 | 2023 | 2024 |
| 1. Strengthen the provision of sanitation services to users. | Index of the Management and Provision of Sanitation Services of the Provider Companies (IGPSS).* | 76.31% | 78.86% | 81.41% | 83.96% | 84.01% |
| | Percentage of providers in rural areas with good management. | 25.05% | 25.88% | 26.72% | 27.56% | 28.41% |
| 2. Consolidate the decentralisation of Sunass functions. | Percentage of ODSs showing optimal performance in the performance of decentralised functions. | 70% | 80% | 90% | 100% | 100% |
| 3. Improve the perception and appreciation of sanitation services by users. | Percentage of users who value the importance of having sanitation services. | 3% | 5% | 10% | 15% | 10% |
| | Percentage of users satisfied with Sunass services | 50% | 55% | 60% | 70% | 75% |
| | Percentage of users of sanitation services who are willing to pay the set tariffs. | 0% | 5% | 10% | 15% | 20% |
| 4. Strengthen Institutional Management | Percentage of internal clients satisfied with the services provided by line bodies.** | 60% | 65% | 70% | 75% | 80% |
| 5. Implement disaster risk management* | Percentage of implementation of Disaster Risk Management Plan. | 50% | 60% | 70% | 80% | 90% |

* The IGPSS is an index composed of 18 indicators spanning six performance areas: access to services; service quality; financial sustainability; governability and governance, and disaster risk management.
** The line bodies refer to the offices within Sunass that provide support and advice, which are the Office of Planning, Budget and Modernization, the Office of Legal Advice, the Office of Communication and Institutional Image, the Office of Administration and Finance and the Office of Information Technologies.

**There is a need for guidance to the public on how indicators can be used to assess the regulator's performance.** In general, it is not clear how target levels are defined, or what the reasons are for changes in these target levels throughout the years. Moreover, indicators may not always be intuitive for the public to understand, where the annual report only reports on the average performance for each strategic objective, which can be based on a number of underlying indicators. For example, it may not directly be clear what is understood to be "good management" of service providers, or what optimal performance in the execution of deconcentrated functions looks like.

*Recommendations*

Short term:

- **Reinstate** the good practice of producing and publishing an annual report on Sunass's activities and performance, an important mechanism to strengthen transparency, accountability and understanding of the regulator's role.

Medium term:

- **Measure** the regulator's performance on its strategic objectives through a set of simple and straightforward performance indicators that are more directly affected by the actions of Sunass, complemented by 'watchtower' indicators on sectoral performance. Indicators more directly affected can include aspects such as the number of providers with an up-to-date tariff study or the number of rural providers that charge a household fee in line with Sunass's methodology. "Watchtower" indicators assess the wider sector performance, and could serve to identify challenges within the sector in order to direct the regulator's actions.

- **Provide** easy-to-understand guidance to stakeholders on the interpretation of key indicators to enable them to track the regulator's performance more easily.

- **Engage** stakeholders in the formulation of target levels for the indicators, and when relevant clearly communicate on the reasoning for any changes made to the target levels (Box 1.16).

---

**Box 1.16. ACCC Performance Consultative Committee**

The ACCC Performance Consultative Committee was established in 2015 to act as the ACCC's formal stakeholder consultation body under the Australian Government's Regulator Performance Framework (RPF), which was in place from 2015 to 30 June 2021. The framework established a common set of six outcomes-based key performance indicators that facilitated assessment of Commonwealth regulators' performance, particularly how they engaged with regulated entities and administered regulations.

In mid-2021 the Government replaced the RPF with the Regulator Performance Guide, which details three principles of regulator best practice:

1. Continuous improvement and building trust: regulators adopt a whole-of-system perspective, continuously improving their performance, capability and culture to build trust and confidence in Australia's regulatory settings.

2. Risk-based and data driven: regulators manage risks proportionately and maintain essential safeguards while minimising regulatory burden, and leveraging data and digital technology to support those they regulate to comply and grow.

3. Collaboration and engagement: regulators are transparent and responsive communicators, implementing regulations in a modern and collaborative way.

---

The committee initially consisted of 16 business, legal and consumer representatives who collectively covered the broad range of stakeholders that the ACCC engages with in undertaking its various functions. In late 2021 it was expanded to just over 20 key stakeholders to reflect the increased breadth of the ACCC's work in recent years, and the expanded scope of the purpose of the committee.

The committee is therefore well placed to continue to provide feedback to the ACCC about its performance.

During its first six years, the committee met annually to:

- provide feedback on the self-assessment methodology, measures, evidence and surveys that the ACCC used to annually assess its performance against the six RPF KPIs;
- 'externally validate' the ACCC's draft annual self-assessment under the RPF.

External validation provided an avenue for the committee to provide feedback on whether the self-assessment results broadly accorded with their views of the ACCC's performance against the KPIs over the assessment period.

With the change to the Regulator Performance Guide, the committee will meet twice per year from 2022 to provide a forum for increased engagement with, and feedback from, key stakeholders on a wider range of performance issues related to the work of the ACCC. This will include our performance in achieving our statutory regulatory obligations and core purpose to 'Make markets work for consumers, now and in the future', as reported through our Corporate Plan and Annual Report.

Sources: ACCC website: https://www.accc.gov.au/about-us/consultative-committees/accc-performance-consultative-committee; information provided by ACCC, 2021.

# Note

[1] For example, energy and mining regulator Osinergmin received PEN 327 million from fees in 2015, compared to the PEN 28 million in fees that Sunass received in the same year.

# References

Felgendreher, S. and P. Lehmann (2015), "Public Choice and Urban Water Tariffs--Analytical Framework and Evidence From Peru", *The Journal of Environment & Development*, Vol. 25/1, http://dx.doi.org/10.1177/1070496515619651.  [3]

OECD (2021), *Implementing Regulatory Impact Assessment at Peru's National Superintendence of Sanitation Services*, OECD Reviews of Regulatory Reform, OECD Publishing, Paris, https://dx.doi.org/10.1787/c0cdc331-en.  [8]

OECD (2021), *OECD Regulatory Policy Outlook 2021*, OECD Publishing, Paris, https://dx.doi.org/10.1787/38b0fdb1-en.  [13]

OECD (2021), *Water Governance in Peru*, OECD Studies on Water, OECD Publishing, Paris, https://dx.doi.org/10.1787/568847b5-en.  [1]

OECD (2020), *Driving Performance at Peru's Transport Infrastructure Regulator*, The
Governance of Regulators, OECD Publishing, Paris, https://dx.doi.org/10.1787/d4ddab52-en. [6]

OECD (2020), *Regulatory Enforcement and Inspections in the Environmental Sector of Peru*,
OECD Publishing, Paris, https://dx.doi.org/10.1787/54253639-en. [11]

OECD (2020), *Regulatory Impact Assessment*, OECD Best Practice Principles for Regulatory
Policy, OECD Publishing, Paris, https://dx.doi.org/10.1787/7a9638cb-en. [9]

OECD (2019), *Driving Performance at Peru's Energy and Mining Regulator*, The Governance of
Regulators, OECD Publishing, Paris, https://dx.doi.org/10.1787/9789264310865-en. [4]

OECD (2019), *Driving Performance at Peru's Telecommunications Regulator*, The Governance
of Regulators, OECD Publishing, Paris, https://dx.doi.org/10.1787/9789264310506-en. [5]

OECD (2018), *OECD Regulatory Enforcement and Inspections Toolkit*, OECD Publishing, Paris,
https://dx.doi.org/10.1787/9789264303959-en. [12]

OECD (2016), *Regulatory Policy in Peru: Assembling the Framework for Regulatory Quality*,
OECD Reviews of Regulatory Reform, OECD Publishing, Paris,
https://dx.doi.org/10.1787/9789264260054-en. [7]

OECD (2012), *Recommendation of the Council on Regulatory Policy and Governance*, OECD
Publishing, Paris, https://dx.doi.org/10.1787/9789264209022-en. [10]

UN-Water (2020), *Peru*, https://www.sdg6data.org/country-or-area/Peru (accessed on
7 July 2021). [2]

# 2 Regulatory and sector context

This chapter provides an overview of Peru's public institutions and describes the main features of the water and sanitation sector as well as the legislative framework that determines the functions of Peru's Superintendencia Nacional de Servicios de Saneamiento (Sunass).

## Institutional framework

Peru is a presidential republic with a unicameral congress (Figure 2.1). The executive branch is represented by a Council of Ministers and the President of the Republic, who acts as head of government and of state. The legislative body is represented by the Congress, which has the power to pass new legislation, to amend and repeal existing law, as well as to approve the state budget. Peru has been experiencing a period of acute political instability in recent years (Box 2.1).

Peru is divided into 26 units, which comprise 24 departments, the constitutional province of Callao and the province of Lima. The province of Lima is independent of any other region, and serves at the country's capital. The other 25 regions have elected regional governments and are in turn divided into provinces and districts.

### Figure 2.1. Peru's public institutions

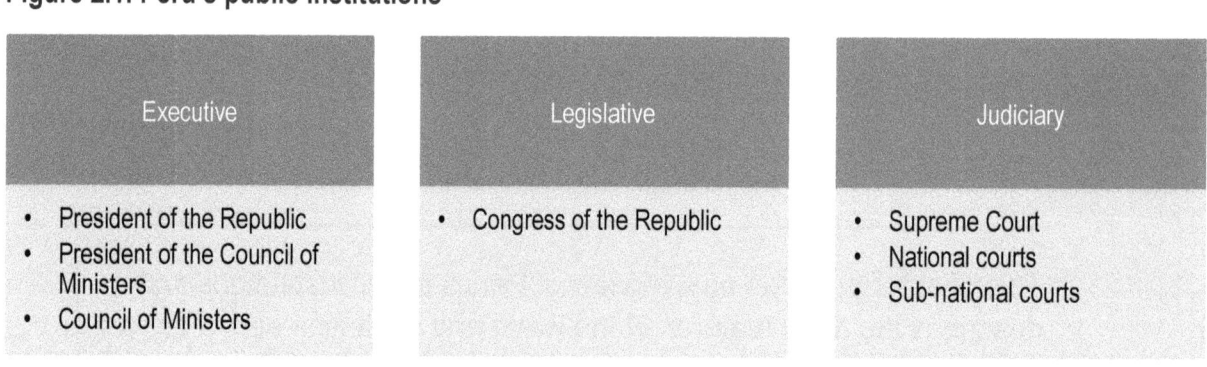

Source: https://www.peru.gob.pe/directorio/pep_directorio_gobierno.asp.

### Box 2.1. Political instability in Peru

Since the beginning of the government of Pedro Pablo Kuczynski in 2016, the country has had five presidents of the Republic and ten presidents of the Council of Ministers. During this period, no president has managed to complete his constitutional term.

This instability began when the first accusations of corruption, linked to the Odebrecht case, were directed at members of the country's political elite. At the same time, economic growth began to slow. The institutional design of government has also led to the formulation of divided governments. From 2016 to date, the dispute between the legislature and the executive has resulted in two resignations of the executive, one dissolution of the congress and one dismissal of the executive.

The frequent changes in administration result in a high turnover of ministerial leadership and staff in the public sector and present a challenge to policy continuity, institutional co-ordination and budget predictability for the regulator.

Source: Ministry of Justice and Human Rights Peru (2019), "Political Constitution of Peru" [Constitución política del Perú], https://www.minjus.gob.pe/wp-content/uploads/2019/05/Constitucion-Politica-del-Peru-marzo-2019_WEB.pdf; World Bank (2021), "GDP growth (annual %) – Peru", https://data.worldbank.org/indicator/NY.GDP.MKTP.KD.ZG?locations=PE; BBC (2020), "Crisis in Peru: 3 keys that explain the political instability in the country" [Crisis en Perú: 3 claves que explican la inestabilidad política en el país], https://www.bbc.com/mundo/noticias-america-latina-54916840.

### Executive branch

The President of the Republic, the Council of Ministers, and the Presidency of the Council of Ministers (*Presidencia del Consejo de Ministros*, PCM) constitute the core bodies of the executive branch (Figure 2.2), (OECD, 2016[11]). Along with the PCM, the Ministry of Economy and Finance (*Ministerio de Economía y Finanzas*, MEF) helps shape the overall regulatory environment in Peru. In the water and sanitation (WSS) sector, the Ministry of Housing, Building and Sanitation (*Ministerio de Vivienda, Construcción y Saneamiento*, MVCS) is responsible for designing sector policies and regulations. Sunass is attached to the PCM as a body with administrative, functional, technical, economic and financial autonomy, alongside the other Peruvian sector regulators (Law No. 27332).

**Figure 2.2. Structure of the executive branch of the Peruvian government**

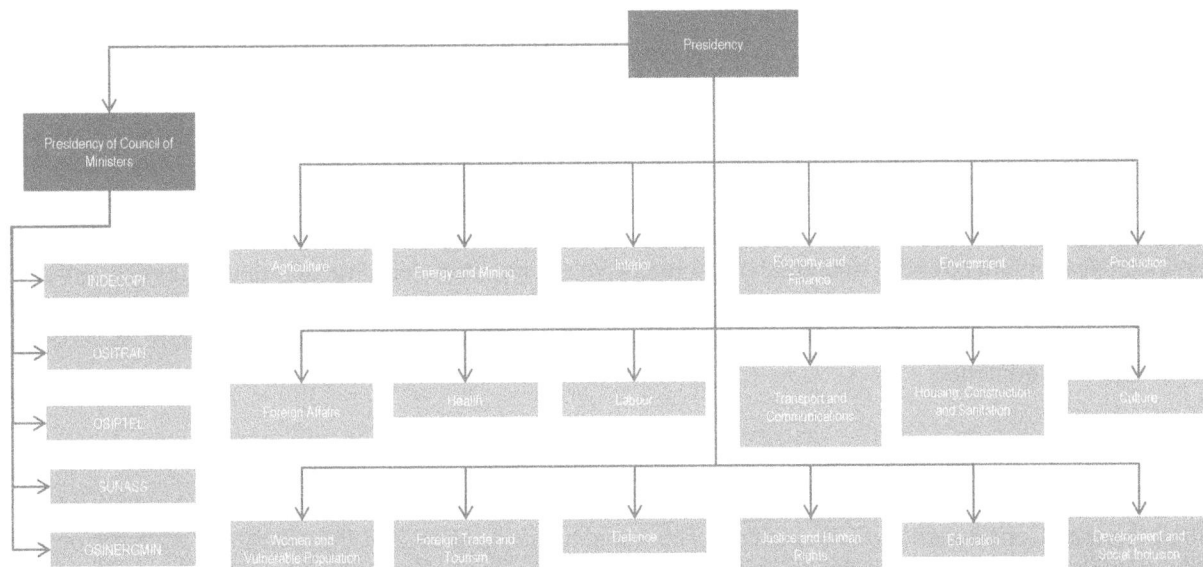

Note: The PCM also houses a large number of public entities, secretariats and commissions, which are not included in this figure.
Source: (OECD, 2016[2]), Regulatory Policy in Peru: Assembling the Framework for Regulatory Quality, OECD Reviews of Regulatory Reform, Paris, http://dx.doi.org/10.1787/9789264260054-en.

#### Presidency of the Council of Ministers (PCM)

The Presidency of the Council of Ministers (PCM) is responsible for co-ordinating national and sector policies within the executive, including line ministries and public agencies. The PCM has legal powers for the modernisation of administration, territorial development, decentralisation, spatial demarcation, public dialogue and social consultation, digital government, communication of the policy actions of the central government and other powers assigned by law. The PCM houses several secretariats and commissions, and manages and co-ordinates line ministries and public entities. The PCM plays a key role in appointing and nominating the Executive President and the members of the Board of the regulator, as well as approving the regulator's strategic planning. While not formally defined in law, the President of the Council of Ministers in practice plays the role of prime minister and government spokesperson (OECD, 2016[1]).

#### Ministry of Housing, Construction and Sanitation (MVCS)

The Ministry of Housing, Construction and Sanitation (MVCS) is the governing body for sanitation as well as housing, construction, spatial development and urban development. It develops, plans, co-ordinates and implements the national policy and direction of the water and sanitation services sector. To do so, it establishes public policies, issues regulations and promotes public-private partnerships (PPPs) in the WSS sector. Sunass works with the MVCS in the implementation of sectoral policies and the development of WSS regulations. Sunass does not intervene directly during the approval process of investment projects in the sector. However, it is charged with the approval of the tariffs of providers, which can affect the viability of investment projects.

### *Ministry of Economy and Finance (MEF)*

The Ministry of Economy and Finance (MEF) is responsible for the development of economic and financial policy in the country and approves Sunass's budget. MEF manages the performance-based budgeting system, which applies to all executive bodies and economic regulators. MEF has a shared responsibility for regulatory policy such as administrative simplification, international regulatory co-operation, inter-governmental co-ordination, performance-based regulation, *ex ante* impact assessments of regulation, and governmental transparency and consultation, co-ordinated together with PCM (OECD, 2016[2]).

### *Agency for the Promotion of Investment (ProInversión)*

The Agency for the Promotion of Investment (*Agencia de Promoción de la Inversión Privada, ProInversión*), created in 2002, is a specialised technical body attached to MEF and is responsible for the promotion of national investments through public-private partnerships in services, infrastructure, assets and other state projects. It provides information and orientation services to investors, mediating different views on investment projects, and creating a conducive environment for attracting private investments, in accordance with economic plans and integration policies, such as those related to the development of transport infrastructure. ProInversión receives technical comments from Sunass when developing concession agreements.

## Legislative branch

The Congress of the Republic is the unicameral body that holds the legislative power, created through the 1993 Political Constitution (OECD, 2016[1]). The constitution dictates that the Congress consists of 130 representatives that are directly elected based on congressional districts allocated to each region (Congreso de la Republica, 2021[3]). Legislation enacted by the Congress can require regulators to develop secondary regulations. The Congress can ask ministries and regulators to issue opinions on draft legislative proposals, and to respond to questions raised by the representatives. The Congress has 24 standing committees, two of which cover the WSS sector: the Commission of Housing and Construction and the Commission of Consumer Protection and Regulatory Bodies of Public Services.

## Sub-national government

Apart from the national level of government, there are three sub-national levels of government: the regional government and two levels of local government (provincial and district local government) (OECD, 2016[1]). The exclusive and joint functions of the different levels of government are described in the Political Constitution, as well as in the Organic Law of the Executive Power (*Ley Orgánica del Poder Ejecutivo –* LOPE), the Organic Law of Regional Governments (*Ley Orgánica de Gobiernos Regionales –* LOGR) and the Organic Law of Municipalities (*Ley Orgánica de Municipalidades –* LOM). Sub-national governments can define regulatory measures within their area. Sunass interacts with the different levels of sub-national government through its decentralised offices.

## Judicial branch

The judicial branch is responsible for the interpretation and application of laws, with the Supreme Court as the country's highest judicial body. This is supplemented by a hierarchical system of 35 superior courts: the National Superior Court of Specialised Criminal Justice and 34 superior courts with a jurisdiction over a judicial district across the 25 administrative regions of Peru. In addition, the tribunals of first instance and the courts of peace (only for minor non-criminal offenses) complete the framework of the judicial system. Sunass decisions relating to complaints, sanctions and tariff approval can be appealed at the administrative tribunals of first instance.

## Sector overview

### *Access to water and sanitation*

According to the Peruvian National Institute of Statistics and Information (*Instituto Nacional de Estadística e Informática* – INEI), 91% of the Peruvian population has access to public water networks, while 77% had access to the public sewerage network. Access differs significantly between rural and urban areas and between the different regions (Figure 2.3). In urban areas, around 95% of population has access to public water networks, against 76% rural areas. Similarly, in urban areas 90% of population has access to public sewerage networks, while in rural areas this is only 28%. Access is most widespread in the region of Tacna, the Constitutional Province of Callao and Lima Province, with an access rate for both public water supply and sewerage well above 90%. Access is least wide-spread in the region of Loreto, with only 56% having access to public water supply and 44% to the public sewerage network (INEI, 2021[4]).

**Figure 2.3. Access to water and sanitation in Peru, 2019**

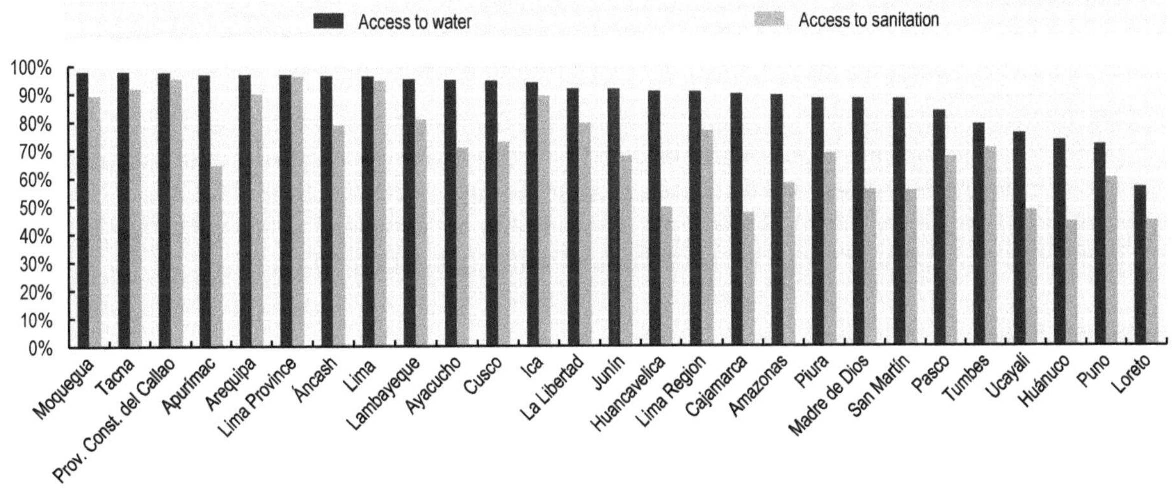

Source: (INEI, 2021[4]).

There are considerable concerns in terms of the quality of the drinking water and sanitation provision in Peru. According to 2020 data on Sustainable Development Goal 6 to "ensure availability and sustainable management of water and sanitation for all", only 51% of population had access to a safely managed drinking water service,[1] while 53% had access to a safely managed sanitation service. Access to at least basic service provision is 93% for drinking water and 79% for sanitation. Similar to the case for overall access to drinking water, access is worst in rural areas – in rural area, only 22% has access to safely managed drinking water services and only 60% has access to at least basic sanitation services (UN-Water, 2020[5]).[2] The percentage of population that consumes water from the public water supply with an adequate chlorine level (≥0.5 mg/l) was 38.7% in 2019 (INEI, 2020[6]).

## *National Sanitation Policy 2017-2021*

In 2017, the MVCS defined a new national sanitation policy for the period 2017-2021, established through Supreme Decree No. 007-2017-VIVIENDA. In practice, the National Sanitation Policy is a progressive layering of successive policies, programmes and initiatives in the sector in the past couple of decades. The policy document defines Peru's objective to achieve universal and sustainable access to sanitation, for urban areas by 2021 and for rural areas by 2030, in accordance with the Sustainable Development Goals (SDGs) (Sanitation and Water for All, 2019[7]). The policy document contains a set of guidelines to improve the management and performance of the sanitation service provision. The objectives are to:

- Increase the coverage, quality and sustainability of sanitation services, in order to achieve universal access.
- Reduce the infrastructure gap in the sector and ensure access to sanitation services, primarily for the rural population and those with limited resources.
- Achieve business autonomy and integration of sanitation service providers.
- Increase the levels of efficiency in the provision of services with high indicators of quality, continuity and coverage.
- Achieve sustainable management of the environment and water resources in the provision of sanitation services.

In order to achieve these objectives, the policy document also includes a diagnosis of the sector. This diagnosis points at insufficient coverage and quality, investment gaps, weaknesses in the management of providers, lack of standards for the formulation of investment projects, a lack of co-ordination between actors and a low public valuation of sanitation services. Based on this diagnosis, it establishes a number of policy axes, which each include a number of more concrete policy guidelines.

Following the National Sanitation Policy, in 2017 a National Sanitation Plan was also enacted. This plan is the instrument for the implementation of the National Sanitation Policy. It identifies and links the necessary actions to achieve the objectives, and discusses in detail the current performance of the sector. Based on this, the plan sets targets for indicators, determines actions and assigns these to sector actors, and defines the investment plan needed to bridge the current investment gap in the sector.

## *Sector structure*

The drinking water and sanitation sector is highly fragmented, with a variety of modes of organisation and operation in the urban and rural areas (Figure 2.4). Fifty publicly owned providers (*Empresas Prestadoras del Servicio de Saneamiento*, EPs) service urban areas with a population higher than 15 000 inhabitants. EPs are responsible for large and intermediate cities, which contain around 62% of the population, or 85% of the urban population (World Bank, 2018[8]). Sunass categorises these EPs by size:

- SEDAPAL, the company that serves Lima, is in a category of its own with over 1 000 000 connections;
- 4 companies with a size between 100 000 and 1 000 000 connections;
- 14 companies with a size between 40 000 and 100 000 connections;
- 15 companies with a size between 15 000 and 40 000 connections; and
- 16 companies with a size below 15 000 connections (OECD, 2021[9]).

Smaller towns with a population between 2 000 and 15 000 inhabitants are serviced by approximately 450 operators. In rural service areas (with fewer than 2 000 inhabitants), service provision is further fragmented. Over 25 000 municipal management units and Sanitation Services Administrative Boards (*Juntas Administradoras de Servicios de Saneamiento* – JASS) manage the water supply and sanitation services (WSS) in rural areas. A JASS is community-based volunteer committee, responsible for the operation of the maintenance of the WSS services and the collection of household fees (OECD, 2021[9]). In total, JASS are responsible for rural areas, and as such are responsible for about 24% of the population, while municipalities (through smaller utilities and municipal management units) are responsible for the service provision to small cities (containing the remaining 14% of population) (World Bank, 2018[8]).

The high number of diverse sector players leads to a loss of economies of scale and raises the problem of resource inefficiencies, as well as bringing significant challenges for regulation and oversight by Sunass (see Assessment and Recommendations). Local authorities have the decision-making power over the merger and consolidation of WSS providers, but there is resistance at the local level for changing the status quo.

Moreover, there is a lack of formalisation of providers in rural areas. Based on a database on 2 854 providers in rural areas (municipal management units and JASS), Sunass found that only 57% were formally established as a provider.[3] For small cities, only 30% of providers were formalised. Formalisation can bring benefits such as the ability to obtain a license for the legal right to use the water resource, the possibility to receive public investment and the right to file a complaint regarding contamination.

**Figure 2.4. Market structure of WSS service providers**

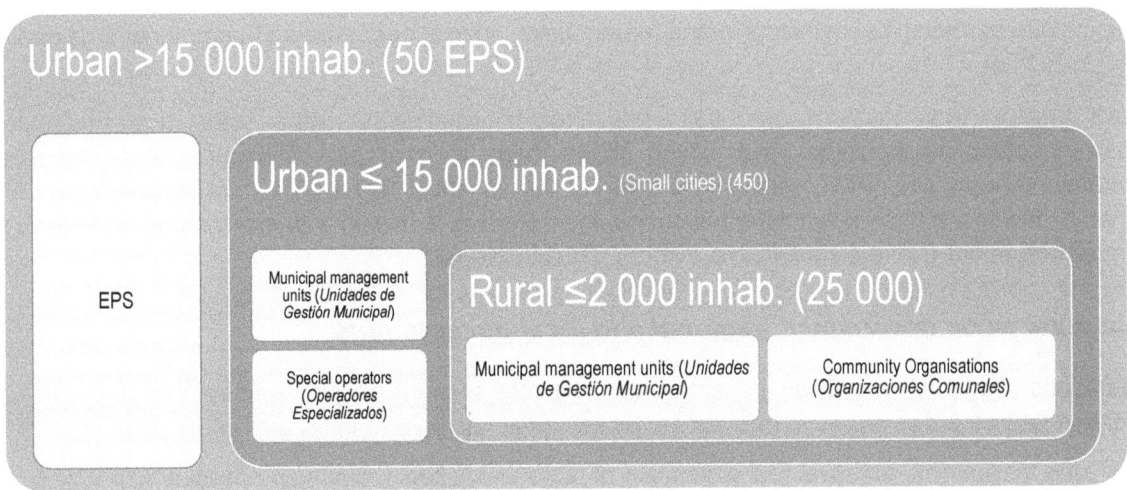

Source: (SUNASS, 2019[10]).

Another key issue for the providers of WSS in Peru is their financial sustainability. Many EPs operate at a loss and rural providers fail to meet basic financial sustainability. Most operators are small public agencies with low income, and often suffering from inefficient management leading to a low quality of the network and high network losses (i.e. leakage). Moreover, the lack of financial sustainability makes many providers unable to invest, leading to a lack of investment in the sector. Prior to the 2016 Framework Law, donated/subsidised assets were not recognised in the tariff setting process, which prevented companies to build up funds for investments in replacement and expansion.

Currently, 19 out of the 50 EPs are included in a "transitory regime" related to a lack of economic and financial solvency, under which management is taken over by the Technical Agency for the Administration of the Sanitation Services (*Organismo Técnico de la Administración delos Servicios de Saneamiento* – OTASS), a state agency attached to the MVCS (Sunass, 2021[11]).

### Tariffs and household fees

Tariffs for EPs, which operate in urban areas with more than 15 000 inhabitants, are set for five-year periods. The tariff methodology takes into account projected demand, costs and investment plans, and aims to ensure economic and financial sustainability of the operator. Tariffs can increase during the period, conditional on the achievement of certain performance targets by the EP. The tariffs also cover payments towards the Ecosystem Services Compensation Mechanism (*Mecanismo de Retribución por Servicios Ecosistémicos* – MERESE). Through these payments, EPs can create reserve funds towards the conservation, recovery and sustainable use of sources of ecosystem services. Similarly, the tariffs also cover payments towards a disaster risk management fund (*Gestión de Riesgo de Desastres* – GRD) and an adaptation to climate change fund (*Adaptación al Cambio Climático* – ACC) (OECD, 2021[9]).

The tariff methodology identifies a number of different consumer categories: residential, commercial, industrial and public. Consumers pay a fixed charge for their water usage, as well as a flexible tariff based on actual consumption. Poor households can make use of subsidised tariffs, which are funded through the tariffs on other users in the system (cross-subsidisation). The Ministry of Development and Social Inclusion (MIDIS) establishes socioeconomic classification of households, on which basis Sunass determines the eligibility of users for subsidies. Following Legislative Decree No. 1280, Sunass is also responsible for determining the methodology for the household fee (*cuota familiar*) for service provision through public-private partnerships, municipal management units, special operators and communal organisations (OECD, 2021[9]).

In rural areas serviced by JASS, users pay a household fee. Sunass has set a methodology for the JASS to use in setting the household fee, which allows them to cover at a minimum the operation and maintenance costs and small replacement costs of the sanitation services in rural areas. While JASS ultimately decide upon the level of the household fees, Sunass is tasked with ensuring the economic and financial sustainability of the sanitation providers (OECD, 2021[9]).

### Multi-level water governance: regional and local governments

Sub-national (regional and local) governments have the responsibility to ensure efficient water and sanitation service provision within their areas. By law, regional governments are responsible for:

- the formulation, approval and evaluation of regional sanitation plans and policies;
- the provision of technical and financial assistance to local governments to support the delivery of water and sanitation services;
- collecting and upgrading data on water supply and sewerage infrastructure and service management indicators (OECD, 2021[9]).

In addition, local governments are responsible for:

- the management of water network assets within the public domain, and granting the exploitation of sanitation services;
- the creation of Municipal Technical Areas (*Área Técnica Municipal* – ATM), which monitor and supervise the service provision by providers and support providers through technical assistance and training (ATMs are not providers, although in some cases they perform a dual function);
- Include the allocation of financial resources for investments in sanitation infrastructure in the Concerted Municipal Development Plans (*Plan de Desarrollo Municipal Concertado* – PDMC) and local participatory budget;
- finance and co-finance investments for the maintenance and replacement of sanitation infrastructure in rural areas;
- collect data and input them into the Water and Sanitation Information System (OECD, 2021[9]).

## Legislation and reforms

### Situation prior to 2013

The Peruvian water and sanitation sector has experienced many reforms in its past. During the 1970s and 1980s, the sector was largely centrally co-ordinated. The General Sanitation Works Service within the Ministry of Housing was in charge of the direction and development of the sector during the 1970s, until in 1981 it was replaced by a large state-owned company that served most of the urban areas of Peru. This company was called the National Service for the Supply of Potable Water and Sewerage Services (*Servicio Nacional de Abastecimiento de Agua Potable y Alcantarillado* – SENAPA), and it included 15 affiliated companies and 12 operating units (Giugale, Newman and Fretes-Cibils, 2006[12]).

Starting from the early 1990s, SENAPA was slowly dissolved, and the companies and operating units were transferred to municipalities. The largest provider from that point was SEDAPAL, which serves the capital of Lima and has remained under the control of the national government. Along with this move towards decentralisation came the creation of Sunass in 1992, in charge of the economic regulation of companies in the sector. Around the same time, in 1992, the Ministry of the Presidency became in charge of sectoral policies. It held this position until 2002, when the ministry ceased to exist. From that point on, it was the Ministry of Housing, Construction and Sanitation (MVCS) that became responsible for sectoral policies in the sanitation sector, to define and implement sectoral policies, formulate development plans and assign investment funds to the sanitation sector (Giugale, Newman and Fretes-Cibils, 2006[12]).

In 1994, the General Law of Sanitation Services (Law No. 26 338) was enacted (El Presidente de la Republica, 1994[13]). The law established that sanitation services are a necessary and public utility of national interest, with the purpose to protect the health of the population and the environment. Provincial municipalities are responsible for the provision of sanitation services, which it can delegate to a provider. It also assigned Sunass with the task to guarantee users the provision of sanitation services of increased quality, contributing to the health of the population and preservation of the environment. The law further specified the regulations regarding the functioning of the sector, such as the rights and responsibilities of service providers, the tariff system and the conditions for private sector participation.

The decentralisation efforts of the 1990s were unsuccessful in achieving universal access, a sustainable sector and efficient autonomous utilities. One reason for this may be that the decentralisation was not accompanied by sufficient capacity building or the necessary incentives for regional and local governments (World Bank, 2018[14]). Tariffs remained at a level that was insufficient for companies to fund investments, as they were hardly able to recover their operational costs. This has led to increased level of indebtedness and the inability to adequately manage the operations related to sanitation provision.

### 2013 Law on the Modernisation of Sanitation Services

Following the General Law of Sanitation Services, in 2013 additional legislation was established through the Law on the Modernisation of Sanitation Services. The purpose of this legislative proposal was to modernise the provision of sanitation services through the establishment of measures to increase access, quality and sustainability, promoting development, environmental protection and social inclusion. The modernisation effort was based on the principles of universal access, social inclusion, protection of the environment, business autonomy and efficiency (El Peruano, 2013[15]).

The 2013 Law of Modernisation of Sanitation Services also created the Technical Agency for the Administration of the Sanitation Services (*Organismo Técnico de la Administración delos Servicios de Saneamiento* – OTASS), attached to the MVCS, but with functional, economic, financial and administrative autonomy and legal status. The law assigned to OTASS to issues rules, guidelines and protocols, promote the merger of EPs, evaluate the technical and economic solvency of companies and contribute to the strengthening of capacities. The law also establishes the conditions under which EPs can be put in a so-called Transitory Support Regime (*Régimen de Apoyo Transitorio* – RAT). EPs can be put in the RAT following an evaluation by Sunass of the company's economic and financial solvency and its compliance with service management indicators and other technical criteria. Sunass can identify through yearly evaluations the companies that should become part of the RAT, while OTASS manages these companies (i.e. elects their board and managers). The RAT is intended as a temporary regime to improve the operations of the EP, with evaluations every three years for EPs included the regime and a maximum duration of the regime of 15 years (Sunass, 2021[11]).

### 2016 Framework Law for the Management and Provision of Sanitation Services

In 2016, the new administration in Peru launched a new sectoral reform initiative, aimed at the achievement of universal access to sanitation services within Peru. The new initiative, established through Law 1280, aimed to:

- Define rules to achieve universal access, quality, efficient performance and sustainability;
- Establish measures to strengthen and increase efficiency in the management of WSS providers;
- Define the roles and functions of authorities responsible for increasing coverage and sustainable provision of WSS throughout the country.

The law sets as key priority the modernisation of the sector through the strengthening of WSS providers. The law aims to transform EPs into public corporations, expected to increase coverage first by including urban areas outside their service area, and subsequently by expanding towards rural areas within their proximity. It establishes the following principles for the provision of sanitation services:

- Universal access;
- The essential nature of sanitation services;
- Social inclusion;
- Autonomy and responsibility in business management;
- Independence in financial resource management;
- Responsibility, transparency and accountability of sectoral entities;
- Good corporate governance and accountability of providers;
- Financial-economic balance;
- Protection of the environment and efficient use of water.

The initiative is expected to increase the incentives for EPs, and also expands the economic regulation of Sunass beyond the EPs to providers in small towns and rural areas. This therefore expands the scope of Sunass's work towards a large number of small providers that it did not work with before. OTASS holds a central role in the transformation of EPs, to promote integration of companies and increase sustainability (Figure 2.5).

Following the 2016 Framework Law and the 2020 Supreme Decree 005-2020-VIVIENDA, Sunass is tasked with implementing a new tariff regulation model for EPs. The tariff model takes into account differences between providers and their ability to face obligations and improve quality, and fine-tunes their tariff regulation accordingly. Companies will be placed on a scale between their initial level of efficiency and the level of efficiency of a so-called model company, based on their level of development.

## Figure 2.5. Activities for the modernisation of WSS sector – Sunass, MVCS and OTASS

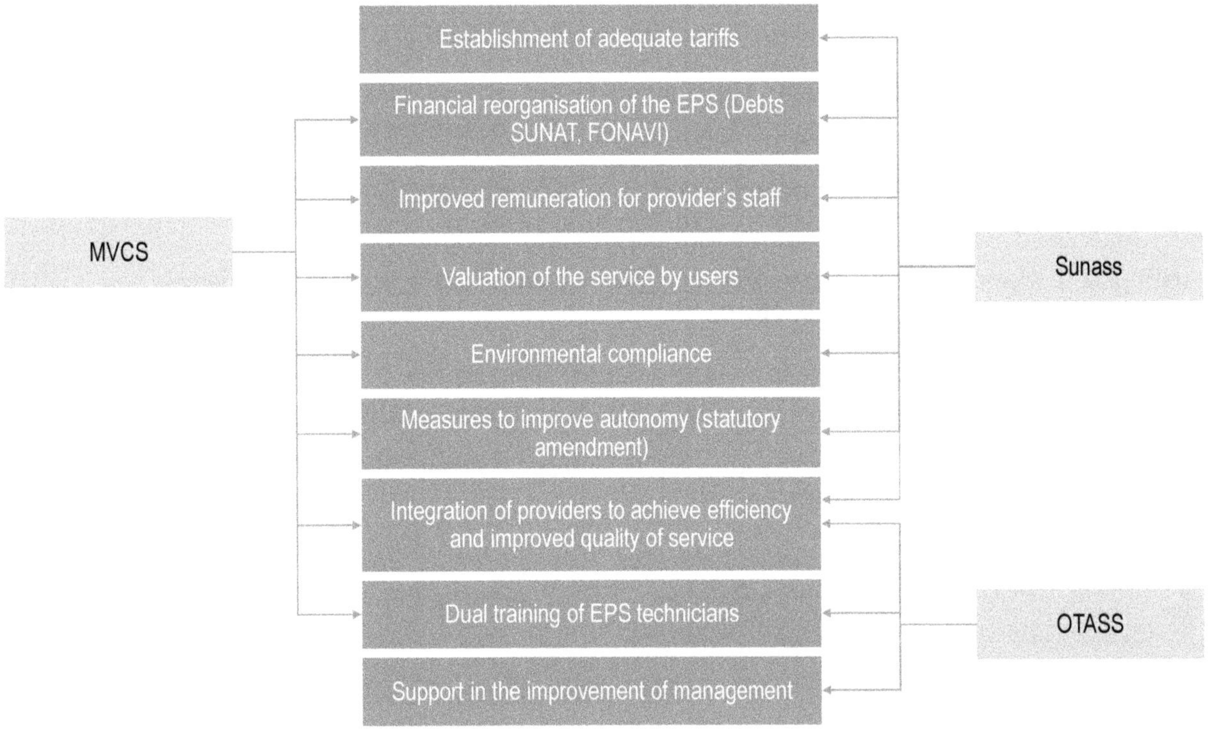

*Source*: Peru: Closing sanitation gaps with evidence-based investments in the sector, Sanitation for All Secretariat, 2019, https://www.sanitationandwaterforall.org/news/peru-closing-sanitation-gaps-with-evidence-based-investments-in-the-sector#:~:text=As%20of%202018%2C%20about%203,7.4%20million%20lack%20sanitary%20sewerage.&text=1280'%20and%20National%20Sanitation%20Policy,of%20sanitation%20sector%20in%20Peru.

## Notes

[1] The population with access to a safely managed drinking water services are considered those with access to "drinking water from an improved water source which is located on premises, available when needed and free from faecal and priority chemical contamination."

[2] The share of rural population with access to a safely managed sanitation service is not specified by the source. The share of rural population with access to at least basic service is with 60% significantly lower than for urban population (84%).

[3] According to the 2016 Framework Law, community organisations are considered formal when they hold an authorisation from the district or provincial municipality. Such an authorisation is granted through a certificate.

## References

Congreso de la Republica (2021), *About Congress*, https://www.congreso.gob.pe/eng/overview/about-congress/.

[3]

El Peruano (2013), *Law of Modernization of the sanitation Services*, [15]
https://busquedas.elperuano.pe/normaslegales/ley-de-modernizacion-de-los-servicios-de-saneamiento-ley-n-30045-951518-1/ (accessed on 8 July 2021).

El Presidente de la Republica (1994), *Ley General de Servicios de Saneamiento Ley No. 26338*, [13]
https://www.sunass.gob.pe/doc/LGSS/ley_26338.pdf (accessed on 8 July 2021).

Giugale, M., J. Newman and V. Fretes-Cibils (eds.) (2006), *An Opportunity for a Different Peru*, [12]
The World Bank, http://dx.doi.org/10.1596/978-0-8213-6862-6.

INEI (2021), *Medio Ambiente*, https://www.inei.gob.pe/estadisticas/indice-tematico/medio-ambiente/ (accessed on 12 July 2021). [4]

INEI (2020), *Perú Formas de Acceso al Agua y Sanaemiento Basico*, [6]
https://www.inei.gob.pe/media/MenuRecursivo/boletines/boletin_agua_junio2020.pdf.

OECD (2021), *Water Governance in Peru*, OECD Studies on Water, OECD Publishing, Paris, [9]
https://dx.doi.org/10.1787/568847b5-en.

OECD (2016), *OECD Public Governance Reviews: Peru: Integrated Governance for Inclusive* [1]
*Growth*, OECD Public Governance Reviews, OECD Publishing, Paris,
https://dx.doi.org/10.1787/9789264265172-en.

OECD (2016), *Regulatory Policy in Peru*, OECD, http://dx.doi.org/10.1787/9789264260054-en. [2]

Sanitation and Water for All (2019), *Peru: Closing sanitation gaps with evidence-based* [7]
*investments in the sector*, https://www.sanitationandwaterforall.org/news/peru-closing-sanitation-gaps-with-evidence-based-investments-in-the-sector.

SUNASS (2019), *Presentation summarising the classification of service providers, as per* [10]
*Supreme Decree No. 019-2017-VIVIENDA", at OECD workshop, Santo Domingo,*
*September.*

Sunass (2021), *Transitory Support Regime (RAT) [Régimen de Apoyo Transitorio (RAT)]*, [11]
https://www.sunass.gob.pe/prestadores/empresas-prestadoras/regimen-de-apoyo-transitorio/
(accessed on 21 August 2021).

UN-Water (2020), *Peru*, https://www.sdg6data.org/country-or-area/Peru (accessed on [5]
7 July 2021).

World Bank (2018), *International Bank for Reconstruction and Development, Project Appraisal* [8]
*Document on a Proposed Loan in the Amount of US$70 Million to the Republic of Peru for a*
*Modernization of Water Supply and Sanitation Services Project*,
https://documents1.worldbank.org/curated/en/118971532835034687/text/Peru-Modernization-PAD-07092018.txt.

World Bank (2018), *The World Bank Modernization of Water Supply and Sanitation Services* [14]
*(P157043)*, https://documents1.worldbank.org/curated/en/706771525142348131/text/Project-Information-Document-Integrated-Safeguards-Data-Sheet-Modernization-of-Water-Supply-and-Sanitation-Services-P157043.txt (accessed on 8 July 2021).

# 3 Governance of Sunass

The Performance Assessment Framework for Economic Regulators (PAFER) was developed by the OECD to help regulators assess their own performance. The PAFER structures the drivers of performance along an input-process-output-outcome framework. This chapter applies the framework to the governance of Peru's water and sanitation services regulator (*Superintendencia Nacional de Servicios de Saneamiento – Sunass*) and reviews the existing features, the opportunities and challenges faced by Sunass.

## Role and objectives

The National Superintendency of Sanitation Services (*Superintendencia Nacional de Servicios de Saneamiento*, Sunass) is Peru's economic regulator for sanitation services, that includes drinking water, sewerage treatment and sanitary disposal of excreta.

The regulator was established in 1992 by Decree Law No. 25965 in tandem with major reforms to the sector that aimed to decentralise and commercialise service provision. Sunass was granted responsibility for overseeing the newly-created municipal Sanitation Service Providers (*Empresas Prestadoras del Servicio de Saneamiento*, EPs) that served urban areas and that were legally and financially separate from municipalities.

In December 2016, a new Framework Law for the Management and Provision of Sanitation Services (from now on: Framework Law 1280) expanded Sunass's role and added a number of functions. Previously, the regulator was responsible for supervising sanitation services in cities with populations over 15 000 inhabitants, which in practice entailed supervising 50 EPs. Framework Law 1280 expanded the scope of the regulator's functions to include the supervision of more than 25 000 service providers in rural areas (known as community-organised water and sanitation services boards, *Junta Administradora de Servicios de Saneamiento*, JASS) and 450 operators in small cities (population between 2 000 and 15 000) to ensure quality of service and financial sustainability. This is a large number of operators to supervise when compared internationally (Figure 3.1).

**Figure 3.1. The number of active water operators in the water and sewerage sector supervised by water regulators**

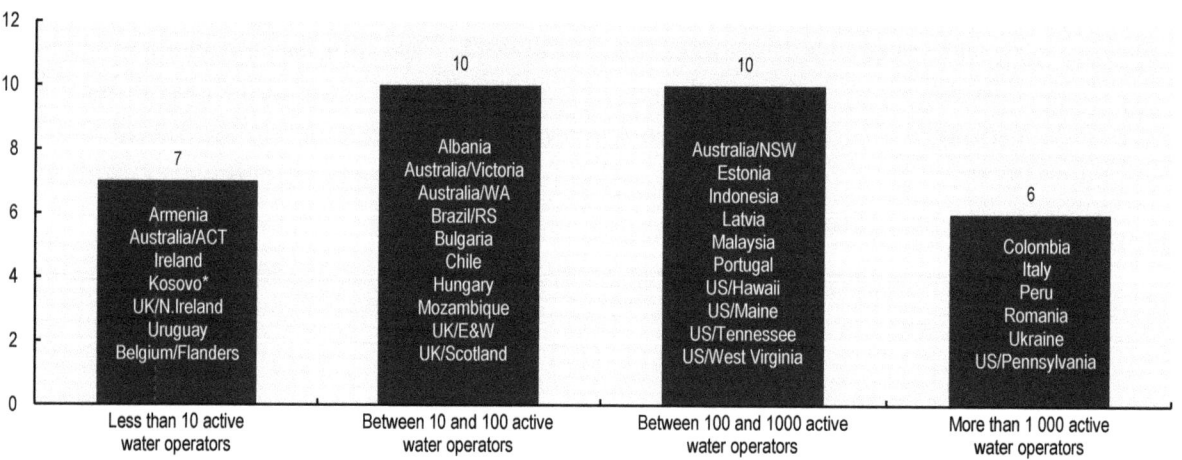

Note: This figure, originally presented in (OECD, 2015[1]) has been updated to reflect the change in category for Peru. Previously Peru was included in the category "Between 10 and 100 active water operators".
* This designation is without prejudice to positions on status, and is in line with United Nations Security Council Resolution 1244/99 and the Advisory Opinion of the International Court of Justice on Kosovo's declaration of independence.
Source: (OECD, 2015[1]).

### *Mandate and objectives*

Sunass's high-level objectives are defined in legislation. The Framework Law 1280 states that Sunass has the responsibility to "guarantee users the provision of sanitation services, in urban and rural areas, under quality conditions, in order to contribute to the health of the population and the preservation of the environment."

## Mission, vision and values

Sunass's mission is to "set tariffs, regulate and supervise the provision of sanitation services by providers in an independent, objective and timely manner, to help citizens ensure the exercise of their rights and duties."[1] The mission statement was approved by the Board of Directors as part of the strategic plan 2020-2023.

Sunass does not have its own vision statement but subscribes to the vision of the Presidency of the Council of Ministers (*Presidencia del Consejo de Ministros*, PCM) to which it is attached, in accordance with the National Center for Strategic Planning (*Centro Nacional de Planeamiento Estratégico*, CEPLAN) guidelines. The vision of the PCM is to be a "Ministry that promotes change, to have a modern, articulated and decentralised State, generating trust in the population and increasing competitiveness".

The regulator's Code of Ethics defines the institutional values as freedom, commitment, trust, cohesion, solidarity, honesty and social responsibility.

## Functions and powers

Law No. 27332 (Framework Law on regulatory agencies for private investment in public utilities, *Ley Marco de los Organismos Reguladores de la Inversión Privada en los Servicios Públicos*, LMOR) grants all Peruvian sector regulators with functions to supervise, set tariffs, issue regulations, inspect the activity of regulated entities, as well as to solve conflicts and claims. Accordingly, Sunass has the following powers:

- Regulatory (*función normativa*): it can dictate regulations, guidance and norms.
- Tariff approval (*función reguladora*): it approves tariffs for the services and activities under its economic regulation.
- Supervisory (*función supervisora*): it supervises the provision of services and evaluates the performance of the companies that provide them. It can verify the compliance of legal, contractual or technical obligations by entities, companies or supervised activities, and verify compliance with any provision, mandate or resolution issued by the regulator.
- Inspections and enforcement (*función fiscalizadora y sancionadora*): it can impose sanctions and corrective measures on service providers for the breach of obligations derived from legal or technical regulations, as well as the obligations of the concessionaires in their respective concession contracts. It has the power to collect fines.
- Claim resolution (*función de solución de reclamos*): it can resolve conflicts that arise between water service operators and users through administrative channels.
- Conflict resolution (*función de solución de controversias*): it can resolve conflicts that arise between companies through administrative channels. In practice, given the lack of competition between providers in the sector, the regulator has never used this power.

In addition to its core regulatory functions, Sunass was given a number of new functions under Framework Law 1280. Sunass has until 2022 to implement the new functions (six years from the enactment of the law). Under the Framework Law 1280, the regulator:

- Determines the geographical area to which utilities are responsible for delivering Water Supply and Sanitation (WSS) services ("service delivery area").
- Approves the efficient scale for the integration of service providers, i.e. it determines the viability of merging service providers to reap economies of scale to become more efficient.
- Grants authorisation to municipalities to provide water and sanitation services in cases where integration with an EP is not possible.
- Supervises the execution of public-private partnership (PPP) contracts linked to the provision of sanitation services.

- Evaluates the EPs according to criteria established in the Framework Law and its regulations, to determine whether they are eligible for the "Transitional Support Regime" under which the Technical Organization for the Administration of Sanitation Services (*Organismo Técnico de la Administración de los Servicios de Saneamiento*, OTASS, the technical body under the Ministry of Housing, Construction and Sanitation, (*Ministerio de Vivienda, Construcción y Saneamiento*, MVCS) assumes management control of the utility.

- Supervises (and sanctions) companies' compliance with legal and technical obligations in relation to accountability, performance and good corporate governance.

- Promotes Mechanisms of Rewards for Ecosystem Services (*Mecanismos de Retribución por servicios Ecosistémicos*, MERESE)[2] by providing technical assistance to EPs on how to calculate and incorporate MERESE into the water tariffs. The regulator is also working with EPs to support the implementation of MERESE funds, exploring the various investment modalities.

An additional function, related to water resources management, was given to Sunass under Legislative Decree 1185/2015. According to this, Sunass establishes and approves the methodology, economic criteria and process for determining the fee for groundwater monitoring and management for sanitation service providers.[3]

In practice, Sunass also provides significant guidance and capacity development (e.g. through trainings and workshops) to service providers and parts of sub-national government (such as Municipal Technical Areas, *Áreas Técnicas Municipales*, ATM) that have responsibilities for overseeing service providers in rural areas. For example, the regulator provides guidance to EPs on disaster risk management and climate change adaptation, so that EPs incorporate these elements in their Optimised Masterplans.

The regulator's functions and powers (Table 3.1) are well understood by the urban EPs, but less so by other service providers. Sunass has long-standing relationships with the 50 EPs that operate in Peru's major urban areas, and these utilities understand the regulator's role in terms of its regulatory functions and its responsibilities for tariff approval, supervision and sanctioning. There is a lower level of awareness of Sunass's functions and powers among the service providers in small urban and rural areas that came under the regulator's supervision in 2017, although Sunass states that this has been improving thanks to information campaigns that it has carried out.

The general public has little understanding of the regulator and its role. According to an Ipsos survey conducted in December 2020 among men and women between 18 and 70 years old in urban and rural areas, only 5% knew Sunass and its duties and 8% knew something about what it does. This means in total only 13% is aware of Sunass.

Furthermore, the regulator reports that it faces resistance to a number of its functions. For example, there is frequent resistance to tariff increases by users and local political leaders – and more broadly resistance to the idea of paying for water as it is perceived a human right rather than a commercial service –, and resistance to efforts to integrate service providers by the EPs, the smaller utilities and consumers.

## Table 3.1. Sunass powers

| Power | Independently done by Sunass | Done by Sunass together with other bodies (e.g. in government) | Not done by Sunass |
|---|---|---|---|
| Regulate tariffs | Yes | -- | -- |
| Propose secondary legislation | Yes | -- | -- |
| Issue guidelines or codes of conduct | No | No | PCM and MVCS (i.e., Corporate Governance Code) |

| Power | Independently done by Sunass | Done by Sunass together with other bodies (e.g. in government) | Not done by Sunass |
|---|---|---|---|
| Investigate cases of breaches in laws or regulations | Yes. For example, when Sunass detects non-compliance in water quality or environmental matters, it sends a report to the competent authorities: General Office of Environmental Health (*Dirección General de Salud Ambiental*, DIGESA) General Office of Environmental Affairs (*Dirección General de Asuntos Ambientales*, DGAA), among others. | No | -- |
| Audit/inspect businesses/other entities on compliance with standards | Yes, for example, the evaluation of financial, technical and administrative issues of the provider companies is carried out, and recommendation reports are issued to the sector to be intervened and included in the Transitional Support Regime (*Régimen de Apoyo Transitorio*, RAT). | No | -- |
| Audit businesses/other entities on measurement, reporting and evaluation | Yes | No | -- |
| Enforce compliance with standards and regulation | Yes | No | -- |
| Impose or ban a particular technology | No | No | The MVCS establishes the construction standards for sanitation infrastructure, enabling the corresponding quality standards to be met. |
| Impose fines or other financial sanctions | Yes, there is a record of sanctions that is published on the Sunass website. | No | -- |
| Impose structural remedies (e.g. structural or functional) | No | No | -- |
| Participate in the planning, maintenance and/or decommissioning of infrastructure | No | No | Provider Companies |
| Collect information from regulated entities and others through compulsory process or voluntary schemes | Yes, through the Data Entry System, which the Inspections Directorate manages. The recording of information is mandatory. | No | -- |
| Publicise benchmarks of environmental standards | No | No | No |
| Provide awards to good performers | Yes, but not as an award but instead as recognition. | No | No |
| Veto the investment plans of operators | Not a "veto", but Sunass evaluates the investment plan submitted for the Tariff Study of the Provider Company. Based on service provision needs and the financial capacity of the company, Sunass determines which projects – in addition to those financed by the MVCS – will be financed by tariffs. | No | -- |
| Issue and revoke licenses | Sunass can grant municipalities with an authorisation to provide sanitation services for a period of three years, in cases where integration with an EP is not possible. After the initial three years, Sunass can renew the authorisation for three more years. It does not have the power to revoke an authorisation. | No | EPs require a law to establish them. Municipal authorities provide licenses to providers in rural areas and small urban areas with a population under 15 000. Ministry of Health (*Ministerio de Salud*, MINSA) and National Water Authority (*Autoridad Nacional de Agua*, ANA) grant authorisations for the dumping |

| Power | Independently done by Sunass | Done by Sunass together with other bodies (e.g. in government) | Not done by Sunass |
|---|---|---|---|
| | | | of wastewater. |
| Mediate to resolve disputes | Yes | No | -- |
| Conduct market analyses | Yes | No | -- |

Source: Information provided by Sunass, 2021.

### Institutional co-ordination

Sunass operates in a complex environment alongside other public bodies at the national and sub-national levels (Table 3.2; Table 3.3).

The Framework Law 1280 defines the respective roles of ministries and other public bodies that intervene in the water and sanitation sector, including Sunass, as well as local and regional governments and service providers. Nevertheless, there appears to be overlap of actions in areas such as data collection, capacity development, and public awareness raising campaigns to promote a "culture of water" and understanding for the need to pay a tariff. Furthermore, different interpretations of Sunass's role by actors in the sector – in particular with regards to responsibilities for ensuring the quality of drinking water – lead to problems of co-ordination. Sunass's definition of service quality for EPs used in its benchmarking indicators does not include water quality, although the definition applied in rural areas does include water treatment (chlorination).

#### Co-ordination at national level

Overall, there is a mismatch between the complex legal framework for the water and sanitation sector and the capacity of Peru's institutions to implement it (OECD, 2021[2]). Low capacity contributes to and is compounded by a lack of clarity around roles and responsibilities as mandates and perimeters of activity are not always clearly understood. There are no regular institutionalised meetings for high-level co-ordination between the regulator and other public authorities that intervene in the water and sanitation sector. Ad hoc meetings between the PCM and Sunass took place in 2020 and the early months of 2021 – framed in particular in the context of the State's response to the COVID-19 pandemic – to discuss issues and to ascertain whether the regulator needed support from the executive. As the co-ordinating body of the executive, the PCM has brokered contacts between Sunass and relevant ministries, notably with the Ministry of Economy and Finance (Ministerio de Economía y Finanzas, MEF) on budgetary issues. The COVID-19 emergency provided the impetus for further ad hoc high-level co-ordination. For example, the MEF convened public authorities in the water sector, including the regulator, to discuss the emergency decree in response to the sanitary crisis.

There are no ongoing or periodic assessments of potential overlaps with other regulatory agencies or gaps in the regulatory framework. However, the Constitutional Tribunal has the power to determine which authority is competent in a particular matter (as stipulated in the Political Constitution of Peru and in the Code of Constitutional Procedure), and the PCM can issue technical opinions on conflicts of competence between entities of the Executive Branch.[4] Competency conflict processes are not common and there has not been a case on this matter in the sector.

To aid co-ordination, Sunass has seven co-operation agreements in place with the following public bodies that commit to exchange of information, technical resources, training etc.:

- National Water Agency (Autoridad Nacional del Agua, ANA)
- OTASS, in the framework of the Modernisation Program with the World Bank

- National Research Institute of Glacier and Mountain Ecosystem (*Instituto Nacional de Investigación en Glaciares y Ecosistemas de Montaña,* INAIGEM)
- Ministry of Environment (*Ministerio del Ambiente,* MINAM)
- National Service of Meteorology and Hydrology of Peru (*Servicio Nacional de Meteorología e Hidrología del Perú,* SENAMHI)
- Energy Investment Supervisory Agency (*Organismo Supervisor de la Inversión en Energía y Minería,* OSINERGMIN)
- Supervisory Body for Private Investment in Telecommunications (*Organismo Supervisor de Inversión Privada en Telecomunicaciones,* OSIPTEL).

## Table 3.2. Co-ordination with other public entities at national level

| Authorities | Type | Scope | Mandate (in relation to sector regulation) | Areas of joint competencies with Sunass |
|---|---|---|---|---|
| PCM | Ministry | National | Co-ordinates national and sectoral policies of the Executive Power. Co-ordinates relations with the other powers of the state, constitutional bodies, regional governments, local governments and civil society. Issues regulations with infra-legal status, such as Supreme Decrees, which may have an impact on the functions of Sunass. | |
| MVCS | Ministry | National | Governing body of the sanitation sector. In charge of establishing and guiding public policies, issuing regulations, promoting public-private partnerships in the industry to provide sanitation services. Carries out technical assistance to service providers in rural areas and small cities. | Co-ordination for the implementation of the sectoral policy. Development of regulations related to the sanitation services sector. Approval of investment programme of the service providers. |
| MINAM | Ministry | National | Co-ordinates the implementation of national environmental policy with the sectors, regional governments and local governments. Approves regulatory provisions within its powers. Formulates and approves plans, programmes and projects within the scope of its sector. Establishes Environmental Quality Standards (EQS) and Maximum Permissible Limits (MPL). Promotes the implementation of mechanisms for the retribution of ecosystem services. | Formulation of regulations related to the protection of natural resources. Recognition in the tariff of the costs of complying with standards and limits. Issuance of provisions aimed at promoting, designing and implementing mechanisms for retribution for ecosystem services. Recognition in the tariff of the amount of retribution for ecosystem services. |
| MINSA | Ministry | National | As the governing body of the Health System, its role is to verify the quality of water for human use. | Definition of provisions and supervises the quality related to sanitation services. |
| DIGESA | Body of the Ministry of Health | National | Formulates and proposes policies on environmental health control and sanctioning. Formulates rules, technical guidelines, methodologies, procedures, protocols and other regulatory instruments related to environmental health control and sanctioning. Regulates the quality of water for human use, water for the population and recreational use. To oversee compliance with current water quality regulations. | Supervision and oversight in matters related to the sector. Recognition in the tariff of the costs of complying with the maximum permissible water limits for human use. |

| Authorities | Type | Scope | Mandate (in relation to sector regulation) | Areas of joint competencies with Sunass |
|---|---|---|---|---|
| ANA | Specialised Technical Agency | National | Manages and monitors natural water sources. Authorises water volumes used and/or distributed by water service providers (EPs and irrigation boards). Evaluates environmental instruments. Grants water use rights (as a natural resource), authorisations for discharge and reuse of treated wastewater. Authorises works in natural water sources (as a natural resource). Manages groundwater in cases where it has not been reserved to water companies. | Issuance of regulations related to water as a natural resource. Supervision on matters related to water as a natural resource. Recognition in the tariff of the cost of water usage. Approval of the tariff for the groundwater monitoring and management service Sunass decentralised offices (ODS) included in technical groups of the Water Resource Councils. |
| OTASS | Specialised Technical Agency | National | Assumes management of EPs that are in the Transitional Support Regime (i.e. that are insolvent). Promotes and implements the sectoral policy regarding the administration and management for the provision of sanitation services. Strengthens the capacities EPs not included in the Transitional Support Regime and other urban service providers. Promotes plans and executes the integration of service providers. Prioritises the entry and management of the Transitory Support Regime in public service providers with municipal shareholding. | Issuance of regulations related to the sanitation sector. Evaluation of the entry or continuity of EPs in the Transitional Support Regime. |
| Private Investment Promotion Agency (*Agencia de Promoción de la Inversión Privada*, PROINVERSION) | Specialised Technical Organization attached to the Ministry of Economy and Finance | National | Executes the National Policy for the Promotion of Private Investment established by the Ministry of Economic and Finance, especially in promoting Public-Private Partnerships. Designs, conducts and concludes the processes of promoting private investment under its scope and the projects entrusted to it and participates in the contractual implementation stage according to its powers. Conducts the processes of private investment in sanitation. | Issuance of opinions on draft concession agreements. |
| National Institute for the Defense of Competition and the Protection of Intellectual Property (*Instituto Nacional de Defensa de la Competencia y de la Protección de la Propiedad Intelectual*, INDECOPI) | Public body attached to the PCM | National | Competition Agency, responsible for resolving disputes related to competition (abuse of dominant position and anti-competitive practices) and bureaucratic barriers. Protects consumer rights. It rules in those cases in which effective injuries to consumers' rights are verified. | Resolution of disputes between users and providers in the second instance. |
| Environmental Assessment and Control Agency (*Organismo de Evaluación y Fiscalización Ambiental*, OEFA) | Specialised Technical Agency | National | Oversees compliance with Maximum Permissible Limits and Water Quality Standards. | Supervision and control of sector-related matters. |
| National Quality Institute (*Instituto Nacional de Calidad*, INACAL) | Specialised Technical Agency attached to the Ministry of Production | National | Governing Body of the National Quality System | Establishment of regulations related to the entities that carry out the subsequent verification of meters. |
| MEF | Ministry | National | Establishes principles, processes, norms, technical procedures and instruments that | |

| Authorities | Type | Scope | Mandate (in relation to sector regulation) | Areas of joint competencies with Sunass |
|---|---|---|---|---|
| | | | guide the budgetary process of public entities. | |
| Ministry of Development and Social Inclusion (*Ministerio de Desarrollo e Inclusión Social*, MIDIS) | Ministry | National | Responsible for the intervention in the rural area of investments in sanitation and maintenance and rehabilitation of the systems. Responsible for the Household Targeting System (SIFOH), which aims to identify people living in poverty, vulnerability or exclusion, as potential beneficiaries of interventions to be provided by social programmes and state subsidies. | |

Source: Information provided by Sunass, 2021.

### Co-ordination at sub-national level

Sunass operates within a complex institutional landscape at the sub-national level, where a number of ministries as well as municipal and regional levels of government intervene in the sector (Table 3.3). Overlaps, duplications and grey areas in regulations and implementation are the consequences of complex relationships across national institutions and levels of governments (OECD, 2021[2]). The unstable political context also presents challenges to co-ordination at this level due to the high turnover in some institutions.

Sunass's decentralised offices lead the co-operation at the sub-national level. Sunass has been described as an open, collaborative and dynamic partner by other public authorities and it identifies co-ordination with other institutions at the sub-national level as an important element to improve effectiveness. The regulator takes part in the Regional Sanitation Commissions, convened by regional governments, which oversee regional sanitation plans. There is also important co-ordination with municipal technical units (ATMs) that are responsible for supervision and enforcement duties until Sunass implements these functions. In particular, Sunass has been providing training to ATMs and rural service providers (JASS/Community Organisations). However, co-ordination can be hindered by the low capacity and high turnover in ATMs.

The degree to which Sunass can co-ordinate with other actors at the sub-national level is also constrained by the relatively limited reach of its decentralised offices. The number of staff and capacity means that the offices face challenges in interacting with all of the large number of municipal governments. Furthermore, while staff from regional governments and ATMs can be on site in local communities, Sunass operates remotely in many cases (e.g. giving virtual trainings) in part due to ways of working in the context of the COVID-19 pandemic, and in part due to resource constraints. Some municipalities are in very remote locations and require significant travel time to reach them. Many of them do not have access to the Internet, excluding them from participating in Sunass's online activities.

There appears to be duplication of efforts by Sunass and other public bodies intervening at the sub-national level, e.g. training service providers, promoting the importance of chlorinated water, and carrying out a stock-taking of water and sanitation infrastructure.

**Table 3.3. Co-ordination with other public entities at sub-national level.**

| Authorities | Type | Scope | Mandate (in relation to sector regulation) | Areas of joint competencies with Sunass |
|---|---|---|---|---|
| Regional governments | Sub-national government | Regional | Responsible for formulating, approving, updating and implementing the Regional Sanitation Plans, carrying out promotional actions, technical assistance, training, scientific and technological research in sanitation. Provide technical and financial support to local | |

| Authorities | Type | Scope | Mandate (in relation to sector regulation) | Areas of joint competencies with Sunass |
|---|---|---|---|---|
| | | | governments to provide sanitation services, in line with the National Sanitation Plan. | |
| | | | Undertake the implementation of sanitation programmes at the local governments' request. | |
| Regional Health Office (*Dirección Regional de Salud*, DIRESA) | Decentralised body of the Regional Government | Regional | Inspects and applies sanctions for non-compliance with the Regulation on Water Quality for Human Use | Control of the process of water treatment for human consumption. |
| Local governments | Sub-national government | Local | Establish a Municipal Technical Area (ATM) to supervise and provide technical assistance and training to service providers in small towns and rural population centres, as appropriate. | The ATM will be responsible for the supervision and enforcement duties until Sunass implements these functions. In the meantime, ATM submits information to Sunass. |
| | | | Participate in the formulation and updating of the Regional Sanitation Plan. | |
| | | | Plan and implement investments to close the sanitation gaps in its jurisdiction, allocate resources for their financing and incorporation in the Regional Sanitation Plans. | |
| | | | Finance and co-finance the replacement and maintenance of rural sanitation infrastructure. | |
| | | | To ensure compliance with sectoral norms. | |

Source: Information provided by Sunass, 2021.

### *International Co-operation*

Sunass has several co-operation agreements in place with development partners (international donors) and non-profit organisations, to support capacity building and provide technical assistance related to the design and implementation of the MERESE payments for ecosystem services scheme. Many of these projects are implemented jointly by Sunass's decentralised offices, while the Office of Planning, Budget and Modernisation (*Oficina de Planificación, Presupuesto y Modernización*, OPPM) in headquarters plays a co-ordinating role, maintaining relations with the Peruvian Ministry of Foreign Affairs (*Ministerio de Relaciones Exteriores*, RREE), the Peruvian Agency for International Cooperation (*Agencia Peruana de Cooperación Internacional*, APCI), other public entities in the sector and international bodies. In addition, it centralises the information regarding the agreements signed by Sunass in a digital tool for internal use.

At the international level, Sunass is active in regional fora and initiatives designed to promote international regulatory co-operation and co-ordination, notably the Association of Water and Sanitation Regulatory Bodies of the Americas (*Asociación de Entes Reguladores de Agua y Saneamiento de las Americas*, ADERASA), and RegWAS LAC (Improvement of Public Policies and Regulation of Water and Sanitation Services Program in Latin America and the Caribbean, *Programa de Mejora de las Políticas Públicas y la Regulación de los Servicios de Agua y Saneamiento en América Latina y el Caribe*).

### Input into policy

Sunass contributes to the formulation and refinement of policies, laws and ministerial regulations by submitting non-binding opinions. During the drafting and approval of a bill, Congress may request Sunass to submit information, comments or suggestions, to which the regulator must respond. A similar situation applies in regulatory projects with infra-legal status, such as supreme decrees issued by the MVCS, to which Sunass may also submit comments.

The regulator creates multidisciplinary teams to prepare the proposed opinions, which are reviewed by Sunass's Policy and Regulations Directorate (*Dirección de Políticas y Normas*, DPN) and the Director of the Office of Legal Advice (*Oficina de Asesoría Jurídica*, OAJ). The workload related to these tasks is deemed to be manageable.

There is no legal requirement for MVCS to request Sunass opinion, although the Single Ordered Text of the Administrative Procedures Law[5] does establish that public bodies should collaborate. On occasion, PCM may convene Sunass and other stakeholders to reach agreement on regulatory texts. In practice, Sunass reports that there have been cases where relevant regulations have been issued by MVCS without prior consultation, or where the regulator has discovered the publication of relevant regulations in the Official Gazette and consequently submitted its comments to these regulations. Sunass has submitted opinions about regulations – including regulations that assign the regulator with new functions – which have not always been taken into account.

Sunass does not publish the opinions and comments it submits. Its comments to Congress are generally summarised in the opinions issued by the congressional committees, and citizens can request the opinions from Congress through the procedure of access to public information.

Sunass also provides opinions on concession contracts overseen by ProInversión, Peru's investment promotion agency. Sunass provides opinions at two points within the investment cycle: its opinion at the "structuring" stage on a first version of the concession agreement is non-binding, while its opinion at the "transaction" stage on a final version of the concession agreement is binding on some aspects, notably regarding the modalities of the agreement related to the definition of rates, access to services, and duties of service providers. Sunass provides opinions that are regarded as technically-sound, but the different priorities of the regulator and the investment promotion agency can result in differences in opinions on contracts. It can take 2-3 rounds to obtain a favourable opinion from the regulator. ProInversión is obligated to publish all information related to projects, which includes Sunass opinions on concession contracts, on its website. In practice, not all Sunass opinions have been published.

At the international level, Sunass contributes to the negotiations of relevant international agreements, for example, the agreements to achieve Sustainable Development Goal 6 on Clean Water and Sanitation.

## Strategic objectives

### Strategic plan

Sunass operates within the framework of a five-year Institutional Strategic Plan (*Plan Estratégico Institucional*, PEI) 2020-2024 that sets out five Institutional Strategic Objectives (*Objetivos Estratégicos Institucionales*, OEIs) and associated goals. The OEIs are intended to contribute to the Sector Strategic Objectives of the Multiannual Sectoral Strategic Plan (*Plan Estratégico Sectorial Multianual*, PESEM) that are set by the PCM. Each strategic objective is linked with quantitative indicators and time-bound goals to enable the regulator to monitor the implementation of the PEI.

The strategic objectives are translated into a Multiannual Operational Plan (*Plan Operativo Institucional Multianual*, POI) that lists all operational activities related to the strategic objectives, to provide coherence between day-to-day activities and the overarching strategic plan. No activity can be undertaken that is not included in the POI.

The regulator has made several changes to its strategic plans in recent years:

- In 2017, the Sunass Board of Directors approved PEI 2017-19, which defined the following OEIs: 1) Optimise the quality of sanitation services provided to users, 2) Contribute to equity in the sanitation services provided to users, 3) Contribute to the rational and sustainable use of water by users and providers of sanitation services, 4) Improve institutional management, and 5) Strengthen disaster risk management.
- In 2019, the Board of Directors approved the PEI for 2017-2022 (in accordance with CEPLAN rules, once the PEI period is established, it can be later extended).

- In 2020, a review of the PEI 2017-2022 determined it was necessary to prepare a new strategic plan.
- In February 2020, the Board approved PEI 2020-23 and changed OEIs 1-3 from the previous plan to those included in Table 3.4.
- In May 2021, the Board extended the PEI to cover 2020-24.

**Table 3.4. Sunass's strategic objectives, indicators and goals, PEI 2020-24**

| Objective (OEI) | Indicator | Goals | | | | |
|---|---|---|---|---|---|---|
| | | 2020 | 2021 | 2022 | 2023 | 2024 |
| 1. Strengthen the provision of sanitation services to the user. | Index of the Management and Provision of Sanitation Services of the Provider Companies (Índice de Gestión de la Prestación de los Servicios de Saneamiento, IGPSS). | 76.31% | 78.86% | 81.41% | 83.96% | 84.01% |
| | Percentage of providers in rural areas with good management. | 25.05% | 25.88% | 26.72% | 27.56% | 28.41% |
| 2. Consolidate the decentralisation of Sunass functions. | Percentage of decentralised offices showing optimal performance in the performance of de-concentrated functions. | 70% | 80% | 90% | 100% | 100% |
| 3. Improve the perception and appreciation of sanitation services by users. | Percentage of users who value the importance of having sanitation services. | 3% | 5% | 10% | 15% | 10% |
| | Percentage of users satisfied with Sunass services | 50% | 55% | 60% | 70% | 75% |
| | Percentage of users of sanitation services who are willing to pay the set tariffs. | 0% | 5% | 10% | 15% | 20% |
| 4. Strengthen Institutional Management | Percentage of internal clients satisfied with the services provided by line bodies. | 60% | 65% | 70% | 75% | 80% |
| 5. Implement disaster risk management* | Percentage of implementation of Disaster Risk Management Plan. | 50% | 60% | 70% | 80% | 90% |

\* This objective is mandatory for all public bodies, as set by CEPLAN.
Source: Information provided by Sunass, 2021.

*Process for setting strategic objectives*

CEPLAN establishes the process and methodology for developing the PEI. Within Sunass, the process is co-ordinated the OPPM.

- Sunass's Executive President forms the Strategic Planning Commission. The ten-member Commission is made up of senior management officials and the heads of the directorates and offices selected by the Board and is led by the Executive President who gives the general points to consider.
- A wider cross-section of Sunass staff are involved in the planning process through the establishment of a technical team (20 members) designated by the Commission and through workshops. In total, around 8% of all staff are involved in the process.
- The technical team prepares a proposed PEI based on the outcomes of workshops that convene senior management and staff from across the organisation, including the heads of the decentralised offices. The Commission approves the PEI document.
- The PEI is sent to the PCM for review and approval. The PCM verifies that the PEI is consistent with the objectives of the sector-wide strategic plan. During the evaluation process of the PEI proposal, the OPPM interacts with the PCM to respond to any queries. To date, Sunass has always received approval from PCM without comments or requests for changes.
- The PEI is sent to CEPLAN for methodological approval.

- The strategic planning process concludes with the approval of the PEI by the Sunass Board of Directors, after which it is published on the regulator's website and the Transparency Portal of Peru.

## Communications

The Office of Communication and Institutional Image (OCII) was created in 2019 to elevate communications to a corporate level with a greater focus on strategic communications with all stakeholder groups to achieve the regulator's strategic objectives. Previously the communications team had been under the Users Directorate and focused on dissemination of information to consumers. The Users Directorate continues to run educational campaigns targeted at consumers.

Sunass has run campaigns to raise awareness on the benefits of drinking treated water and designed communications approaches to support the acceptance of paying for water. The decentralised offices have staff trained in communications to support the strategy designed in the headquarters. A lack of budget however means that in practice there are few local campaigns and that people working on the campaigns are unpaid. Plans to roll out further campaigns were put on hold during the COVID-19 pandemic to focus all communication on the sanitary emergency.

Sunass recently modified its website to be more user-focused, using simple and accessible language. In addition, Sunass prepares information materials using plain language and some communication pieces are prepared in native languages.

## Independence and preventing undue influence

Law No. 27332 establishes Sunass as a public and decentralised body attached to the PCM with administrative, functional, technical, economic, and financial autonomy. Sunass produces its annual work programme independently. The regulator nevertheless depends on the PCM or MEF for approval of several procedures:

- Budget [MEF]
- Strategic Plan (PEI) [PCM and CEPLAN]
- Staff Assignment Chart (*Cuadro para Asignación de Personal*, CAP): the classified positions of the entity based on the current organic structure provided for in its Regulation on Organization and Functions [PCM]
- Analytical Staff Budget: the budget for the specific services of permanent and temporary staff. [MEF]
- Standards, except for regulations, which must undergo a regulatory quality analysis.[6] [PCM]
- Permission for international travel by staff. [PCM]

## Input

### Financial resources

Sunass is financed by a mix of government funds and fees from industry. The reform of the regulator's mandate in 2016 changed its financing model. Previously the regulator was funded solely by fees from the utilities it regulated, collecting a maximum of 1% of annual turnover after sales and promotion taxes.[7] To cover the expansion of its mandate outside of urban areas, government funds now provide the majority of the budget while the income from regulated entities represents 42% of its annual budget (Table 3.5).

Government funds are transferred directly from MEF to Sunass at the start of the calendar year in the form of budgetary credits. Utilities pay the fee to Sunass on a monthly basis (49 out of 50 providers comply with payment of fees).

## Table 3.5. Sources of revenue

| Source of revenue | 2015 | | 2016 | | 2017 | | 2018 | | 2019 | | 2020 | | 2021 | | 2022 (est.) | |
|---|---|---|---|---|---|---|---|---|---|---|---|---|---|---|---|---|
| | Amount (mln PEN) | % of total funding | Amount (mln PEN) | % of total funding | Amount (mln PEN) | % of total funding | Amount (mln PEN) | % of total funding | Amount (mln PEN) | % of total funding | Amount (mln PEN) | % of total funding | Amount (mln PEN) | % of total funding | Amount (mln PEN) | % of total funding |
| Government funds | 0 | 0 | 0 | 0 | 27.9 | 48 | 52.7 | 66 | 64.1 | 61 | 68.5 | 65 | 55.5 | 58 | 53.1 | 63 |
| Fees | 27.8 | 100 | 29.8 | 100 | 30.8 | 52 | 27.4 | 34 | 41.1 | 39 | 37.2 | 35 | 40.3 | 42 | 31.2 | 37 |
| Resources from Official Credit Operations | | | | | | 0 | | 0 | | 0 | 0.2 | 0 | 0 | 0 | 0 | 0 |
| Total | 27.8 | 100 | 29.8 | 100 | 58.6 | 100 | 80.1 | 100 | 105.2 | 100 | 105.9 | 100 | 95.8 | 100 | 84.3 | 100 |

Source: Information provided by Sunass, 2021.

Sunass's total budget rose to PEN 105.9 million (approximately USD 26 million) in 2020, 3.5 times larger than its budget in 2016, in line with the expansion of its duties. However, since then, the government contribution to the budget has decreased. As a result, the budget decreased by nearly 10% to PEN 95.8 million in 2021, and is expected to decrease by another 12% to PEN 84 million in 2022, driven also by an expected drop in revenues from fees. The regulator asserts that its resources are insufficient to carry out its mandate. Even before the expansion of its functions to rural areas, Sunass considered that its budget was inadequate to carry out its functions fully, as water utilities in Peru tend to be small public agencies with low business income. Although the 1% cap applies to all regulatory agencies, water sector income is vastly different from other sectors (e.g. energy and mining).

Underfinanced activities include supervision/inspection (in particular, the supervision of PPP contracts, funds and reserves and the inspection of wastewater treatment processes and water quality standards) and tariff-setting (new tariff regulation requires more frequent tariff updates and tariff-setting in small cities). The regulator signals that activities such as data collection and information management, as well as equipment, software and the maintenance of information systems are also underfinanced.

### *Managing financial resources*

The execution of expenditure is carried out by budget period from 1 January to 31 December, based on the institutional budget approved each year following rules issued by the MEF (Table 3.6).

The budget process is co-ordinated with the MEF through a digital system. Sunass submits information via the online Integrated Administrative Financial System (*Sistemas Integrados de Administración Financiera*, SIAF) every day as part of Peru's administration-wide performance based budgeting system.

Sunass carries out multi-annual budgeting as part of its strategic planning process. The OPPM oversees the preparation of the budget:

- Co-ordination meetings are held with the teams in Lima and the decentralised offices to prepare the POI and the Multiannual Budget Programming and Budget Formulation.
- The POI is drawn up within CEPLAN guidelines and the operational activities and physical goals are determined.
- Once the POI is defined, the multi-annual budget is prepared according to budgetary regulations.

- Each Sunass office/team completes a table of needs for the operational activities under their responsibility.
- The table of needs is assessed by OPPM and the budget is determined.
- The expected income level and the budget execution of the previous year are taken as a reference.
- To ensure alignment of Sunass budget with the PEI objectives, every POI activity is aligned with a strategic objective, and related financial information is recorded.
- The budget is submitted to the MEF for approval.
- In the case of payroll or administrative contracting of services (*Contratación Administrativa de Servicios,* CAS) personnel, the MEF uses the number of positions recorded in its Software Application for the Centralized Record of Payrolls and Human Resources Data of the Public Sector (*Aplicativo Informático para el Registro Centralizado de Planillas y de Datos de los Recursos Humanos,* AIRHSP) as a parameter.

## Table 3.6. Annual budget by area (2021)

| | Certification of Budget Credit (000s PEN) | % of allocated budget |
|---|---|---|
| Management of decentralised offices | 24 304 | 27.4% |
| Administrative management | 20 068 | 22.6% |
| Supervision and enforcement of sanitation services | 13 973 | 15.7% |
| Communication and user service | 9 181 | 10.3% |
| Regulation and tariff fixing | 7 630 | 8.6% |
| Resolution of claims and disputes | 4 010 | 4.5% |
| Development of regulatory tools | 2 830 | 3.2% |
| Superior driving and orientation | 2 752 | 3.1% |
| Planning and budgeting | 1 701 | 1.9% |
| Technical and legal advice | 1 477 | 1.7% |
| Administrative sanctioning procedure – Infractions and Sanctions Commission (CIS) | 593 | 0.7% |
| Control and audit actions | 337 | 0.4% |
| Total | 88 856 | 100% |

Notes: The certification of the budget credit is an administrative procedure whose purpose is to guarantee that the budget credit will be available for the respective fiscal year, in order to authorise expenditure according to the institutional budget. The allocated percentage was obtained by averaging the Opening Institutional Budget (*Presupuesto Institucional de Apertura,* PIA) and the Modified Institutional Budget (*Presupuesto Institucional Modificado,* PIM). PIA: 88,856,348; PIM: 95,761,514.
Source: Information provided by Sunass, 2021.

The OPPM produces weekly reports on budget execution. Each month there is an opportunity to review and re-align, if necessary, the allocation of resources across different units, following the review of budget execution and compliance with the prioritisation of operational activities.

As with other public bodies under the aegis of the PCM, Sunass records all its financial operations in SIAF. Information on Sunass's revenues and budget is available on the publicly accessible MEF portal "*Transparencia Económica Peru*" and updated daily. Furthermore, Sunass has progressively adhered to international quality standards for financial management and in 2020 achieved ISO certification (ISO 9001:2015).

Sunass is bound by several central government rules with regard to managing its financial resources:

- The budget is approved yearly by the MEF before approval by Congress.

- Staff members of Sunass are remunerated according to minimum and maximum limits fixed by Supreme Decree and endorsed by the Council of Ministers and the MEF.
- The PCM has approval authority in some instances, for example, the approval of trips abroad for institutional representation.
- Surplus funds from fees can be carried forward to the following year(s), while any surpluses from the government funds must return to the Treasury every year. Sunass has encountered difficulties in resource allocation due to earmarking of its different revenue streams. Government funds are intended to be used solely for Sunass's new responsibilities in small cities and rural areas. However, some personnel carry out functions in larger urban areas as well as small cities and rural areas.

Moreover, Sunass reports that initially it encountered issues due to the allocation of the national budget, where its budget allocation was distributed through the MVCS rather than directly from MEF. Late receipt of the budget led to insufficient funds for the regulator to pay salaries, causing delayed payments and a number of labour disputes. The regulator reports that it now receives funds directly from MEF, which has improved the process.

Internal audit is assured by an Institutional Control Body (*Órgano de Control Institucional*, OCI) that is part of the Comptroller General of the Republic (*Contraloría General de la República del Perú*, CGR), the highest authority of the National Control System (*Sistema Nacional de Control*, SNC), who supervises, monitors and verifies the correct application of public policies and the use of resources of the state and assets. The purpose of the OCI is to oversee spending and the transparent management of resources at the regulator. The OCI is responsible for auditing all public spending, for example, by monitoring the procedures and evaluation process related to contracts, procurement and other services. The regulator assesses that scrutiny by OCI has increased in recent years.

The head of OCI is appointed by and reports to the Comptroller's office, as officially the Comptroller's office is represented within the regulator through the chief auditor of OCI. The head of the OCI is paid from the budget of the CGR while the other OCI staff salaries are paid with public resources from Sunass.

OCI reports are submitted to the Comptroller General and the Executive President or General Manager of Sunass. Most reports cover financial activities. Some examine Sunass operational activities (e.g. purchase of vehicles for decentralised offices or inspection of Sunass assets) or verify the supervision and inspection activities of different decentralised offices or decisions of the Administrative Tribunal for the Settlement of Sanitation Users' Claims (*Tribunal Administrativo de Solución de Reclamos de los Usuarios de los Servicios de Saneamiento*, TRASS). OCI reports are available online.

### Human resources

Sunass has a total workforce of 630 staff. (Table 3.7, Table 3.8). The total workforce grew by 23% between 2017 and 2020. This trend was driven largely by an increase in the number of staff in support and advisory offices,[8] which more than doubled over the period.

### Table 3.7. Sunass staff by category, 2017-2020

| Year | Staff in support and advisory offices | Staff in directorates | Total Workforce |
|------|---------------------------------------|-----------------------|-----------------|
| 2020 | 137 | 493 | 630 |
| 2019 | 107 | 459 | 566 |
| 2018 | 94 | 456 | 550 |
| 2017 | 53 | 434 | 487 |

Source: Information provided by Sunass, 2021.

**Table 3.8. Sunass staff by department, 2020**

| Body | Unit | 2020 | | | | | | Total | |
|---|---|---|---|---|---|---|---|---|---|
| | | CAP | % | CAS RDR | % | CAS RO | % | | |
| Service Delivery Area Directorate | Lima (HQ) | | | | | 34 | 5.4% | **34** | 5.4% |
| | Regional offices | 7 | 1.1% | 69 | 11.0% | 184 | 29.2% | **260** | 41.3% |
| Inspection Directorate | | 16 | 2.5% | 5 | 0.8% | 28 | 4.4% | **49** | 7.8% |
| Policy and Standards Directorate | | 7 | 1.1% | 5 | 0.8% | 10 | 1.6% | **22** | 3.5% |
| Tariff Regulation Directorate | | 15 | 2.4% | 6 | 1.0% | 15 | 2.4% | **36** | 5.7% |
| Sanctions Directorate | | 2 | 0.3% | 2 | 0.3% | | 0.0% | **4** | 0.6% |
| Users Directorate | | 5 | 0.8% | 15 | 2.4% | 12 | 1.9% | **32** | 5.1% |
| General Management | | 3 | 0.5% | 1 | 0.2% | 2 | 0.3% | **6** | 1.0% |
| Administration and Finance Office | | 12 | 1.9% | 13 | 2.1% | 30 | 4.8% | **68** | 10.8% |
| Legal Counsel's Office | | 5 | 0.8% | 2 | 0.3% | 2 | 0.3% | **9** | 1.4% |
| Internal Control Office | | 1 | 0.2% | 2 | 0.3% | 2 | 0.3% | **5** | 0.8% |
| Communications and Institutional Image Office | | 4 | 0.6% | 8 | 1.3% | 2 | 0.3% | **14** | 2.2% |
| Office of Planning, Budget and Modernization | | 1 | 0.2% | 2 | 0.3% | 11 | 1.7% | **20** | 3.2% |
| Information Technology Office | | 1 | 0.2% | | 0.0% | 22 | 3.5% | **23** | 3.7% |
| Executive President's Office | | 5 | 0.8% | | 0.0% | 3 | 0.5% | **8** | 1.3% |
| TRASS | | 17 | 2.7% | 23 | 3.7% | | 0.0% | **40** | 6.3% |
| TOTAL | | 104 | 16.5% | 153 | 24.3% | 373 | 59.2% | **630** | 100% |

Note: RO = resources from government budget; CAS = Administrative Service Contracting (Contratos Administrativos de Servicios), Law 1057 regime; CAP-P = Cadre for Assignment of Provisional Staff (Cuadro para Asignación de Personal Provisional), Law 728 regime.
Source: Information provided by Sunass, 2021.

Sunass's Organisation and Duties Handbook (*Manual de Organización y Funciones*, MOF) and Organisational Duties Regulation (Reglamento de Organización y Funciones, ROF) outline the main functions of each position. Any changes to the ROF requires approval by the PCM via a Supreme Decree.

### Staff composition

Sunass staff come from a wide range of professional and academic backgrounds, with engineers as the largest group, followed by lawyers and economists (Table 3.9). The regulator also counts on a significant number of staff with communications, management and accounting backgrounds. Anecdotal reports from Sunass suggest that a significant portion of Sunass staff have worked in other regulators. About 10% of Sunass's functions and duties are carried out by contractors and external consultants.[9]

**Table 3.9. Sunass staff**

| Job family | Number | Percentage |
|---|---|---|
| Engineering | 159 | 24.7 |
| Law | 124 | 19.3 |
| Economics | 83 | 12.9 |
| Communication Science | 58 | 9.0 |
| Management | 47 | 7.3 |
| Accounting | 40 | 6.2 |
| Biology | 33 | 5.1 |
| Technicians | 33 | 5.1 |
| Non-specified profession | 30 | 4.7 |

| Job family | Number | Percentage |
|---|---|---|
| Sociology | 14 | 2.2 |
| Education | 4 | 0.6 |
| Psychology | 3 | 0.5 |
| Political Sciences | 2 | 0.3 |
| Geology | 2 | 0.3 |
| Social work | 2 | 0.3 |
| Tourism and gastronomy | 2 | 0.3 |
| Anthropology | 1 | 0.2 |
| Architecture | 1 | 0.2 |
| Librarian and Information Science | 1 | 0.2 |
| Trade | 1 | 0.2 |
| Statistics | 1 | 0.2 |
| Physics | 1 | 0.2 |
| Operations Research | 1 | 0.2 |
| | 643 | 100 |

Note: Information as of March 2021.
Source: Information provided by Sunass, 2021.

Women are under-represented in the organisation at senior management level (Table 3.10), although women form the majority on the Board of Directors. Overall, women make up 46% of total staff and just over half of technical staff.

## Table 3.10. Staff gender balance

| Staff category | Female | Male |
|---|---|---|
| Senior management | 4 | 12 |
| Technical staff | 152 | 148 |
| Support staff | 145 | 182 |
| Total | 301 | 342 |

Note: Information as of March 2021. Senior Management comprises the Board of Directors, the Executive President and General Management.
Source: Information provided by Sunass, 2021.

Looking ahead to the next ten years, the regulator has identified the need to strengthen capabilities in the areas of data management and data science, and in obtaining and managing biophysical information in the watersheds and its impact on the economic aspects of regulation, to support the regulator's new role in the MERESE processes.

### Recruitment

Sunass recruits most personnel in accordance with the rules and procedures established by the National Civil Service Authority (*Autoridad Nacional del Servicio Civil*, SERVIR) and the Ministry of Labour and Employment Promotion (*Ministerio de Trabajo y Promoción del Empleo*, MTPE). The official employment website, managed by SERVIR, publishes information on each stage of the process from selection to the final results. There are no pre-established criteria for recruitment. General Management gives the final approval on recruitment for each post.

Sunass has 18 posts that are considered "positions of trust" (*puestos de confianza*) that are exempt from the public merit-based competition.[10] The law allows free appointment and removal for this type of personnel and the minimum requirements for the posts are defined in the Sunass job classifier. Positions of trust are designated in the CAP-P. The positions of trust are General Management, several Directors[11]/Head of Offices and advisors to the Executive President and General Management.

Sunass cannot hire staff at managerial level directly from a regulated entity. There is a one-year pre-employment cooling-off period. Post-employment restrictions are also in place for higher levels of staff and include a one-year cooling-off period during which these staff members cannot work for a regulated entity. Both restrictions appear in article 80 of the Supreme Decree No. 017-2001-PCM.

### Remuneration and contract conditions

Sunass public servants work under two different employment regimes: Laws No. 728 and No. 1057. Fourteen per cent of staff work under labour regulations for the private sector, not commonly offered in public entities (Law No. 728 regime).[12] Law No. 728 offers open-ended contracts with full benefits. The number of positions is fixed, meaning that recruitments under the Law No. 728 regime can only be made when a Law No.728 position has been vacated. Agencies under this labour regime have remuneration scales that are different from the single remuneration system. It enables highly qualified personnel in positions of responsibility to be exempt from the requirement of advancing step-by-step through an organisation's levels of hierarchy. Directors of Offices/Departments who are recruited via public competition are under this regime.

86% of Sunass employees are hired under the Law No. 1057 regime for CAS. The CAS regime offers fewer employment benefits, such as insurance or pensions, in contrast to the 728 regime. However, Law No. 29849 established the progressive elimination of Law No. 1057, and Law No. 31131 granted labour rights to employees under this regime.

For staff that are in "positions of trust" (e.g. the General Manager, the advisers of the Executive President, certain Directors), their appointment is not subject to a term and can be terminated at any time and without reason of cause.

Sunass follows the remuneration schemes according to the two employment regimes noted above. Sunass staff is not eligible for performance-based pay. Any changes to salary bands within a specific remuneration regime require approval from the Ministry of Economy and Finance and must comply with the Law of Budget and Budgetary Balance. However, Sunass internal regulations do afford staff some additional benefits, such as a day off on a staff member's birthday.

Sunass salaries are considered competitive when compared to salaries in regulated companies in the water and sanitation sector. However, Sunass reports that its salaries are on average lower than those in other regulators in Peru. Sunass does not keep track of salary gaps for comparable positions in the regulated sector.

### Training and talent retention

Sunass has a People Development Plan (*Plan de Desarrollo de las Personas*, PDP) based on training needs expressed by Sunass teams and that is in line with the institutional strategic objectives. For technical work such as tariff studies, new staff take on average 2-3 years to be able to prepare a tariff study autonomously. Their skills are developed primarily through on-the-job training and support from the team.

Staff turnover appears relatively high, averaging 17% per year from 2017-2020 (Table 3.11). Several stakeholders note that Sunass turnover is however lower compared to ministries, as the regulator's staff is more sheltered from political changes than the executive. Informal exit surveys carried out by Sunass's HR office indicate that staff leaving Sunass tend to move to the executive, either the PCM or other ministries. Talent retention can be difficult as career progression can be slow. There is currently no strategy or guidelines for talent retention.

### Table 3.11. Turnover of staff, 2017-2020

|  | 2017 | 2018 | 2019 | 2020 |
|---|---|---|---|---|
| Turnover % | 18 | 20 | 18 | 13 |

Source: Information provided by Sunass, 2021.

### *Performance evaluation*

In 2021, Sunass introduced a performance evaluation system for the first time. The system follows the guidelines and criteria established by the SERVIR. Under these guidelines, performance appraisals are carried out by senior officers. Feedback is not sought from others apart from the staff's supervisors/managers, such as clients or external partners. Staff are not invited to comment on the performance of their supervisors and managers on a systematic basis, although the SERVIR guidelines do allow for this possibility. The results of the first staff performance evaluation will be available at the end of 2021/early 2022.

## Internal organisation and management

Headquartered in Lima, Sunass has 24 decentralised offices (*Oficinas Descentralizadas*, ODS), one in each region of the country except for the region of Ancash which has two ODS.

The internal structure of Sunass (Figure 3.2) is defined in its ROF, which was updated in 2019 (by Supreme Decree No.145-2019-PCM in its first section and by Presidential Resolution No. 040-2019-SUNASS-PCD in its second section) to adapt to its new functions. Any changes to the internal structure of the regulator requires approval by the PCM. In the face of reticence on the part of PCM to create new teams as reported by Sunass, the regulator has operated within these constraints and on occasion created functional teams within Directorates (i.e. at the level where Sunass can make changes).

### *Management*

Sunass has three senior management bodies: the Board of Directors, the Executive Presidency and General Management. The role of each Senior Management body is established in the ROF.

- The Board of Directors: The highest governing body of Sunass, in charge of establishing objectives, institutional policy and regulatory decision making. It interacts with the Executive President, General Management and the different administrative bodies of Sunass in the approval of initiatives or documents.

- Executive President: The highest executive authority of Sunass is responsible for supervising the implementation of the decisions of the Board of Directors. They are the head of the entity and carry out the management and representation duties of Sunass. They interact with the Board of Directors, the General Management and the different administrative units of Sunass, reviewing initiatives or documents for approval by the Board of Directors. Five staff work in the Executive Presidency.

- General Management: Sunass's highest administrative authority. It is responsible for the administrative and operational management of Sunass by the internal and line administration bodies and the implementation of the decisions of the Board of Directors the Executive President. It serves as the Technical Secretariat to the Board of Directors. It interacts with the Board of Directors, the Executive President and the different bodies of Sunass, reviewing and presenting initiatives or documents for approval by the Executive President and the Board of Directors. It also oversees the different bodies under its responsibility – five Offices and six Directorates – directing and supervising the administrative and operational management of Sunass. General Management also represents Sunass in judicial proceedings. Five staff work in General Management.

In total, there are 46 managers in Sunass, across all organisational levels from the executive management level, to heads of offices/directorates, to heads of unit. The Board of General Management convenes 18 managers and aims to aid interaction and co-ordination across offices and directorates.

## Figure 3.2. Sunass organisational structure

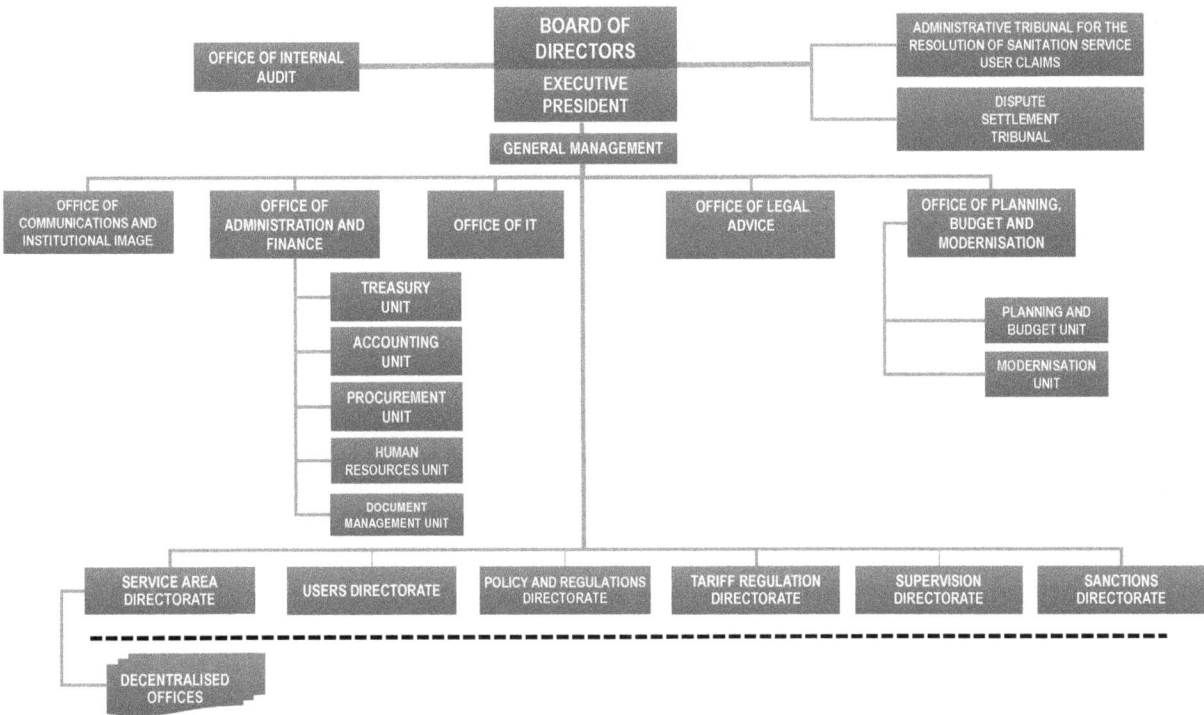

Source: Information provided by Sunass, 2021.

*Teams*

The description of the responsibilities of each administrative unit is established in the ROF:

- The Policy and Regulations Directorate (*Dirección de Políticas y Normas*, DPN, 22 staff) is responsible for developing Sunass regulations (norms), carrying out regulatory impact analysis and undertaking studies and research aimed at strengthening the regulatory system.
- The Tariff Regulation Directorate (*Dirección de Regulación Tarifaria*, DRT, 36 staff) is responsible for evaluating and proposing the rates, prices and quality of sanitation services provided by the 50 urban service providers every five years. The DRT also determines the management goals for each utility.
- The Service Area Directorate (*Dirección de Ámbito de la Prestación,* DAP, 313 staff) is responsible for determining the areas of provision of sanitation services (both the current and potential area that EPs should serve). The team also provides technical assistance to EPs on mainstreaming disaster risk management and climate change adaptation, and advises on the estimation of MERESE that EPs propose to incorporate into tariffs. DAP also oversees the decentralised offices. DAP has been training the decentralised offices to carry out several functions (e.g. technical assistance, fieldwork needed to determine the areas of service provision).

- The Supervision Directorate (*Dirección de Fiscalización*, DF, 45 staff) is responsible for verifying compliance with legal, contractual or technical obligations by sanitation service providers.

- The Sanctions Directorate (*Dirección de Sanciones*, DS, 5 staff) is responsible for evaluating, determining and imposing sanctions on companies (providers of sanitation services, as well as directors and managers of companies that provide sanitation services) in the event of non-compliance with legal and technical obligations or the decisions of Sunass. It was created in 2019 as part of the new organisational structure.

- The Users Directorate (*Dirección de Usuarios*, DU, 33 staff) is responsible for assisting and guiding the users of sanitation services and for co-ordinating stakeholder engagement processes.

- The Office of Planning, Budget and Modernisation (*Oficina de Planificación, Presupuesto y Modernización*, OPPM, 17 staff) is the advisory body responsible for the processes of strategic planning, budgeting, investment, modernisation, and international co-operation. It defines management indicators to monitor and evaluate institutional plans and policies. It co-ordinates budget planning, execution and evaluation. It produces the regulator's annual report. The modernisation unit is responsible for a number of initiatives such as administrative simplification, process management, quality standards, knowledge management, continuous improvement and organisational structure. The international co-operation team is in charge of international negotiations with Sunass's international partners to conclude agreements, projects and activities.

- The Office of Legal Advice (*Oficina de Asesoría Jurídica*, OAJ, 9 staff) is the advisory body responsible for issuing opinions and advising on matters of a legal nature to Senior Management and to the units. It provides legal advice on regulatory issues (e.g. reviews PPP contracts in order to prepare Sunass's institutional opinion) and also on internal affairs e.g. reviewing contracts that Sunass signs, ensuring legal conformity of the Board's decisions, responding to Freedom of Information requests.

- The Office of Communications and Institutional Image (*Oficina de Comunicaciones e Imagen Institucional*, OCII, 15 staff) is the advisory body responsible for strategic communications and media relations.

- The Office of Administration and Finance (*Oficina de Administración y Finanzas*, OAF, 68 staff) is divided into five teams covering accounting, treasury, procurement, human resources and document management.

- The Office of IT (*Oficina de Tecnologías de Información*, OTI, 24 staff) is responsible for IT infrastructure, governance, information management and co-operating with other organisations in the sector on common initiatives.

- The Administrative Tribunal for the Resolution of Sanitation Service User Claims (*Tribunal Administrativo de Solución de Reclamos de los Usuarios de los Servicios de Saneamiento*, TRASS, 42 staff) is the autonomous technical body that exercises the decision-making function of Sunass with respect to claims of a commercial and operational nature between users and service providers. It has a Technical Secretariat in charge of providing legal and administrative technical support.

- Office of Internal Audit (*Órgano de Control Institucional*, OCI, 4 staff) is part of the CGR, the highest authority of the SNC, who supervises, monitors and verifies the correct application of public policies and the use of resources of the State and assets. The purpose of the OCI is to oversee the spending and transparent management of resources at the regulator. The OCI is responsible for all auditing all public spending; for example, by monitoring the procedure and evaluation process related to contracts, procurement, and other services.

*Decentralised offices*

The 24 ODS were established in 2017. Most offices have a standard structure of eleven people: a head of office, two supervision specialists (in some offices there may be three to five supervision specialists), an environmental management officer, social manager, an economic analyst, an administrative assistant, a communications officer, two user relations officers and a driver.[13] Sunass has identified that this structure may need to change given the heterogeneity of the regions and their different needs.

Sunass is pursuing a strategy of progressively decentralising functions to the ODS. As of 2021, the decentralised offices are responsible for supervision, enforcement, service delivery area determination (in co-ordination with DAP in headquarters), and user engagement. In 2022, the regulator is due to decide which other functions will be decentralised. The focus of their work has changed in the four years since they were established. Originally efforts were directed at rate regulation (calculation and application of the "household fee" in rural areas) and oversight, the offices are now more focused on inspections.

The ODS report to the DAP. While hierarchically and functionally the ODS depend on DAP, the offices also receive guidelines on how to carry out their functions from the Supervision Directorate and the Users Directorate. All communications between the ODS and headquarters are channelled through the Head of Office. Sunass is in the process of building capacity within the ODS and the offices require substantial support and guidance from the directorates in headquarters.

The 24 ODS are organised into four macro regions to help standardise administrative processes and channel requests from headquarters. Each ODS can communicate its needs directly to DAP or to their macro region. A meeting between all ODS and senior management takes place weekly. In addition, *ad hoc* meetings between the Directorates in headquarters discuss what is required from decentralised offices.

## Process

### Governing body and decision making

Sunass has a five person Board of Directors. The Board is represented on a full-time basis by the Executive President. The Executive President exerts executive and administrative functions, ensuring the implementation of Board decisions, and reports on behalf of the regulator to the PCM and MEF. The other four members of the Board exert their duties on a part-time basis. Members are remunerated about PEN 1 500 (EUR 320) per session of the Board, but extraordinary meetings are unpaid. Members may be employed by other public institutions intervening in the water sector.

*Board selection*

The Framework Law No. 27332 establishes the requirements for Board membership. Board members must:

- be a professional with at least ten years of practice.
- have recognised professional solvency and suitability, defined as at least three years of experience in an executive management position (i.e. decision-making authority in public or private companies); or five years of experience in matters within the regulatory agency's jurisdiction; and,
- have completed a master's level degree in matters related to the activity within the competence of the regulatory agency.

The selection process (regulated by Supreme Decree No. 103-2012-PCM) is carried out through a public contest managed by a Selection Committee composed of the following members:

- Two members proposed by the PCM, one of whom presides and has the casting vote;

- One member proposed by the MEF; and,
- One member proposed by the MVCS.

At the end of the evaluation stage, the Selection Committee submits to the President of the Council of Ministers the list of selected candidates (no more than three) for each member of the Board of Directors. The President of the Republic chooses among the candidates from the list presented by the PCM. If the President of the Republic disagrees with the list of selected candidates, they may request a new procedure. The selection process can be lengthy, resulting in vacant Board seats for a period of time.

The Executive President must also sit a written exam, set by the PCM and designed by a university, as part of their recruitment process.

Board members are appointed for a five-year term by the Supreme Decree signed by the President of the Republic and endorsed by the President of the Council of Ministers. Board members can present themselves for a new contest and be re-elected after their initial term is complete.

The terms of Board members are staggered: every year a Board member ceases their term and a new member is appointed. Board terms are calculated from the expiration of the mandate of the previous member, regardless of when the new member is appointed. Therefore, if a member is elected late, they will not serve the full five years but rather will complete the remaining time.

Given the part-time nature of the role, Board members may be employed elsewhere, including in other organisations that have a role in the WSS sector, although members are not allowed to work for sanitation companies (regulated entities) during their term or one year prior to taking up office.

To mitigate against potential conflicts of interest, the General Regulations of Sunass listed in the supreme decree No.017-2001-PCM, stipulate that the Board of Directors must submit a Sworn Statement of Interests at the beginning and the end of their term and each year. Furthermore, Law No. 27588 sets out prohibitions and incompatibilities of public officials, civil servants and persons rendering services to the State. The Selection Committee decides whether any conflicts of interest would prevent a candidate from taking up a Board position.

### Decision-making by the Board

In accordance with the ROF, the Board has responsibility to:

- set Sunass's strategic direction (approves the strategic plan and budget)
- take regulatory decisions and actions (exclusive authority of Board, no delegation of regulatory decision-making)
- monitor performance
- approve annual report
- approve internal policies
- ensure compliance with the law and with the organisation's constitutions and policies
- review appeals
- appoint the members of the Dispute Settlement Tribunal (*Tribunal de Solución de Controversias*, TSC) and approve the members of the TRASS.

The Board meets twice a month to discuss the issues submitted for its decision. The annual operational plan sets out the number of scheduled regulatory and tariff decisions for the year ahead, which provides visibility to Board members. Nevertheless, extraordinary meetings can be called if the two monthly Board meetings are not sufficient to take decisions within prescribed deadlines (e.g. to issue an opinion on a concession contract). Extraordinary meetings are called on average every two months.

Decisions are made collectively. Members reach consensus on most decisions; very few decisions go to a vote. In the case of a tied vote, the Executive President has the casting vote. There is no differentiated mandate or division of labour between Board members. Rules governing decision-making by the Board are not codified in an operational manual or guidelines.

According to the ROF, Sunass's General Management acts as the Technical Secretariat to the Board. All regulatory proposals and other documentation prepared for the Board by the technical directorates passes through General Management before it is presented to the Executive President and then the Board. General Management chairs "pre-Board" meetings in order to settle any points of contention between the different directorates and to collect feedback from other directorates on proposals. The OAJ provides legal advice to the Board and provide comments on legal aspects on all regulatory proposals. General Management is also responsible for ensuring the correct implementation of the Board's decisions.

The Board makes decisions based on the information prepared by Sunass directorates. The Board receives the agenda and supporting documents three days before its meetings, and no new information can be introduced during the Board meeting itself. The Board interacts with technical staff from the directorates during Board meetings, during which a representative of the technical team will present and explain the proposal. It is rare for the Board to reject a regulatory or tariff proposal. However, directorates are occasionally required to expand their reports, submit new information or evaluate additional aspects of proposals, upon request by the Board.

Board decisions are published in the official gazette (*El Peruano*) and on the regulator's website. The information that the Board uses for decision-making is also disclosed on the website once the decision has been made and published. Sunass opinions on concession contracts are sometimes but not systematically published on ProInversion's website.[14]

Proposals for regulatory changes are generally triggered by Sunass directorates raising concerns about specific regulations.

### *Regulatory quality tools*

#### *Ex ante assessments and ex post reviews*

Sunass has been receiving technical assistance from the Organisation for Economic Co-operation and Development (OECD) on the implementation of Regulatory Impact Analysis (RIA) to align with international best practice that has resulted in new internal guidelines for RIA that were approved in 2021. Prior to this, the regulator's evaluation of draft regulation relied mainly on a limited approach to cost-benefit analysis and there was no proportionality requirement to tailor the level of the assessment to the potential impacts of the new regulation. The assessment and the regulatory proposal were regularly but not systematically sent to other managers in Sunass for comment, before being presented to General Management and then the Board of Directors for approval.

Under the new internal guidelines for RIA, the DPN is responsible for conducting *ex ante* assessments for each regulatory proposal. Under the new system, the *ex ante* analysis will focus mainly on costs and benefits of proposed regulation, incorporating both quantitative and qualitative criteria. The methodology enables the regulator to consider alternatives to regulations (including no regulation) during the design of regulations.

There is currently no assigned internal unit with a responsibility to check the quality of *ex ante* assessments.

The regulator does not carry out *ex post* reviews of the regulations it issues.

### *Inspections and enforcement*

Sunass applies different compliance and enforcement approaches depending on the type of service provider.

#### *Legal framework*

The General Administrative Procedure Law establishes the obligations and rights of the parties involved for inspections and enforcement. In addition, two further regulations establish the rights and obligations of parties involved and contain principles that guide the exercise of the oversight function:

- The General Regulation on Supervision and Sanctions establishes obligations and rights of the parties involved (Provider Companies, Managers and Directors) for urban EPs.
- The Regulations for the Supervision of Communal Organisations establish obligations and rights of the parties involved (Communal Organisations and Municipal Management Units) for rural areas.
- The regulation for the supervision of service providers in small towns is under development.

#### Service providers in urban areas (EPs)

According to the Framework Law No. 1280, Sunass supervises and has the power to sanction water and sanitation service providers in urban areas. In particular, Sunass supervises:

- Good corporate governance: includes compliance with the standards of the Code of Good Corporate Governance, compliance with bylaws, corporate transformation, the procedure for the appointment of general managers and directors, among others. This is a relatively new topic to be supervised (introduced via the Framework Law No. 1280).
- Commercial aspects: includes the procedure for access to the service, application of the tariff structure, prices of collateral services, billing modality, the content of receipts, billing quality control, meters, closing and reopening, attention to complaints from users of sanitation services, modalities of remote attention due to the national state of emergency due to COVID-19, attention to appeals, and attention to general commercial problems.
- Technical-operational aspects: inspection of wastewater treatment processes, compliance with Maximum Allowable Values (MAV) regulations for non-domestic wastewater, compliance with maintenance programmes for the sewage system (networks, collectors, pumping stations), application of pressure calculation methodology and continuity of service.
- Complaints against the service providers depending on their area of competence (related to the provision of sanitation services, good corporate governance).
- Control of drinking water treatment processes, operational reliability, reservoir cleaning and maintenance programme, drinking water treatment plant, sampling frequency when applicable (if the provider company already has a Quality Control Plan (*Plan de Control de Calidad del Agua*, PCC), the Health Authority is in charge of supervising the sampling frequency).
- Compliance with management goals established in the tariff studies.
- Establishment and use of the investment fund and reserves for Payment for Ecosystem Services (*Pagos por Servicios Ecosistémicos*, PSE), Disaster Risk Management (*Gestión del Riesgo de Desastres*, GRD), Adaptation to Climate Change (*Medidas de Adaptación al Cambio Climático*, ACC), PCC, the sanitation adequacy programme (*Programa de Adecuación Sanitaria*, PAS), as established in the tariff study prepared by the Tariff Regulation Directorate.
- PPP contracts as established in the contract within the scope of Sunass's jurisdiction.[15]

- Supervision of Directors and Managers: Requirements and impediments to holding the position of Chief Executive Officer; Requirements and impediments for the performance of the position of Director; and compliance with the obligations of the Framework Law by Directors and Managers.

**Service providers in rural areas**

Sunass has chosen not to sanction providers in rural areas for an initial period of two years, after which this approach will be reassessed. The regulation stipulates that the supervision approach is to inspect and provide guidance and recommendations rather than sanctions. The regulator is trying to create incentives for suppliers to comply through benchmarking providers and publicising good practices among peers, and a system that recognises "efforts to improve" rather than compliance. Furthermore, roughly 50% of service providers are informal and therefore not subject Sunass's sanctioning powers. In rural areas, Sunass supervises: access, monitoring of quality, control of the water treatment (chlorination) process, operational reliability, monitoring of the sewage disposal process, application of the methodology for calculating the household fee, collection, recording of information, closures and re-openings, as set out in the Regulation on Quality of Sanitation Service Provision.

Supervision is carried out by Sunass's decentralised offices or the ATMs within municipal governments. ATMs report needing to visit JASS/Communal Organisations on a frequent basis due to high rates of non-compliance. For example, water is often not treated and JASS do not cut supply in cases of non-payment. Formal Communal Organisations have two years to comply with access, closures and re-openings and collection requirements. Informal Communal Organisations are issued with recommendations.

As part of the monitoring process, Sunass identifies good practices by Communal Organisations on specific themes (which since 2018 has been water treatment). These good practices are promoted in regional workshops with other communal organisations.

The process for supervising and providing guidance to providers in rural areas will be in place until May 2022, when it will be evaluated under the Regulations for the Supervision of Communal Organisations, and a decision will be taken whether to continue or not with this approach.

**Service providers in small cities**

Regulation for the third category of service providers – those based in small cities – was under development at the time of writing and scheduled for final approval by the end of 2021. The proposal does not suggest sanctioning providers in case of non-compliance.

*Inspection planning*

Sunass carried out 503 inspections of EPs in 2020, of which 111 were triggered by complaints from users about operational aspects (Table 3.12). Every complaint is followed up by the regulator. If Sunass determines that the complaint has been dealt with by the provider company, the procedure is concluded and the user is informed. If Sunass concludes that the complaint was not addressed, an inspection is triggered and the results are reported to the complainant. It can take some time for an inspection to take place after a complaint. For example, among the 111 inspections carried out in 2020 due to complaints, some of these related to complaints made in 2018 and 2019. Sunass reports that breaches are most frequently related to control of treatment processes, operational aspects and quality of billing.

ODS started carrying out inspections in response to complaints in June 2020. Prior to this, all inspections were carried out by the Supervision Directorate.

## Table 3.12. Inspections, 2020

|  | Total |
|---|---|
| Total number of inspections | 503 |
| *Inspections due to complaints* | 111 |
| Planned inspections (at the initiative of Sunass) | 392 |
| Corrective measures (breaches) | 364 (68 reports) |
| Corrective measures implemented | 109 (18 reports) |
| Corrective measures non-implemented (beginning of sanctioning procedures) | 255 (50 reports) |

Source: Information provided by Sunass, 2021.

An Annual Inspection Plan is included as part of Sunass's POI. Sunass considers several pieces of information and data to establish the inspection plan, including:

- Providers' performance in the previous year (management indicators on service quality in the case of EPs; ATMs assessment of the providers' management in the case of rural providers);
- Whether imposed corrective measures (for EPs) or recommendations (for providers in small cities and rural areas) from the previous year were implemented; and
- (For EPs only) Complaints received and resulting actions by the EPs.

Based on this information, an analysis of strengths, opportunities and threats is carried out to identify risks. Risks are rated and the type of supervisory actions that are needed to mitigate the risks are established. Finally, the plan takes into account the assigned budget ceiling and available resources.

The ODS define their own inspections schedule which is incorporated by the Supervision Directorate into the overall proposed inspection plan that is sent to the Board for approval as part of the POI. Once the POI is approved, the annual inspection plan is approved by the General Manager.

Sunass's ODS implement the annual inspection plan with oversight from headquarters. Each ODS has at least one supervision officer. The ODS benefit significantly from the supervision and enforcement expertise in Lima. The Supervision Directorate does not have access to the complete information on inspections held by the ODS.

Some regulated entities are still supervised directly by the Supervision Directorate in headquarters, in particular in cases where there is no need to go on site or where files were started before the ODS were set up.

The outcomes of inspections are shared with the service provider. They are not published on the Sunass website, although anybody can request to see an inspection report.

The rate of non-compliance with imposed corrections is relatively high at 60-70%. Furthermore, the COVID-19 pandemic exposed several irregularities with EPs (e.g. tariff studies not up to date, lack of investment funds) that suggest high rates of non-compliance with Sunass regulations.

The Supervision Directorate performs an *ex post* audit of its decisions (to verify validity) twice a year.[16] Sunass does not currently review enforcement and inspection aspects during the development of new regulations.

A report by the OCI in 2020 highlighted the insufficient capacity of Sunass's Supervision Directorate to carry out all its functions.

*Operational co-ordination*

A number of other authorities have inspection and enforcement responsibilities in the sector:

- The Health Authority monitors drinking water quality[17] (compliance with Maximum Permissible Limits, MPL) and Sunass supervises the monitoring of the water treatment process by EPs (i.e. Sunass does not monitor water quality in the distribution networks, this is done by the Health Authority).
- If a company has a PCC, the Health Authority supervises the frequency of water testing; if it does not yet have a PCC, Sunass supervises the testing frequency.[18] The PCC includes the parameters to be monitored, the monitoring points in the water supply systems for human consumption, and the frequency. 17 out of 50 EPs have PCCs.
- Regarding wastewater treatment, Sunass supervises the monitoring of treatment processes by EPs. The DGAA in the MVCS, supervises compliance with the MPL of discharges, in line with its role at the environmental control entity of sanitation services (within the framework of Law No. 29325, Law of the National System of Environmental Assessment and Oversight).
- MINAM supervises compliance with environmental quality standards in water bodies (rivers, lakes etc.).
- ANA issues authorisations for wastewater discharge and drinking water treatment.

A report by the OECD in 2020 on the Environmental Evaluation and Enforcement Agency of Peru (*Organismo de Evaluación y Fiscalización Ambiental* – OEFA), noted a need for OEFA for strengthened co-ordination, clarity on the distribution of mandates and tasks and more systematic data sharing among institutions (OECD, 2020[3]).

*Enforcement*

Enforcement decisions are taken by the Enforcement Directorate, with no involvement of the Board of Directors. Regulated entities have up to 15 working days to appeal a sanction. Enforcement decisions are published on the regulator's website.

Sunass may apply written warnings, fines and removal orders for directors and managers of utilities. The General Rules on the Supervision and Sanction of Sanitation Services Companies specifies whether a written warning or fine is applicable, depending on the type of breach. The amount of the fine varies depending on the type of provider company, the particularities of the breach and the avoided or postponed costs. The amount of the fine can be reduced by up to 50% in case of early payment and admission of wrong-doing. Fines are differentiated according to the type of provider company:

- Type 1: up to 15 000 total potable water connections.
- Type 2: From 15 001 to 150 000 total potable water connections.
- Type 3: From 150 001 to 1 000 000 total potable water connections.
- Type 4: More than 1 000 000 total potable water connections.

This sanctioning regime was made more lenient during the state of emergency for the COVID-19 pandemic. If firms could show that their revenues had decreased by more than 20% then the fine was replaced with a written warning.

According to the regulator, monetary sanctions had limited success in changing the behaviour of companies. The Framework Law No. 1280 introduced the possibility to remove managers and directors, a measure that Sunass uses in cases where management does not meet legal requirements to hold their position or in case of conflict of interest.

*Compliance promotion*

Sunass differentiates between activities to promote compliance and activities to enforce compliance with laws or standards. Compliance promotion activities in EPs include:

- Regulatory benchmarking of EPs (using indicators, identification and promotion of good practices, recognition of good practices).
- Guidance sessions on the application of regulations (especially important in the context of high turnover of personnel in the EPs).
- Workshops on good corporate governance supervision guidelines (representatives from the MVCS and OTASS are invited).
- Monitoring EPs: verification of regulatory compliance with regulations that are not yet applicable is carried out, and recommendations are made for improvement by the EPs of possible non-compliance. The advantage of monitoring is that it has been possible to warn of possible non-compliances, that the EP can then correct.

Compliance promotion activities for rural providers (mostly Communal Organisations) take a similar approach, including benchmarking, identification and sharing of good practices (based on indicators and/or noted during inspections), rewards for good practice.

## Engagement and transparency of engagement process

*Stakeholder consultation*

Engagement with regulated entities and other stakeholders is provided for under legislation. Tariff setting and any regulatory framework reforms are subject to stakeholder consultation, with different processes followed for each. Sunass does not yet carry out public consultations for tariffs in smaller urban areas (the regulatory scheme is currently being designed) or in rural areas, where communities set the household fee.

### Consultation on tariffs

According to the Tariff Regulation, the EPs propose a "tariff structure" and Sunass conducts the tariff study with the final formulation of the tariff. Sunass presents EPs with a draft tariff study that includes a proposal of tariffs (rate formula and rate structures that will be applied by the EP), management goals and the investment plan of projects to be financed by tariffs for each five-year regulatory period.

Sunass submits the draft tariff study to public opinion and comment by the EP through publication in the official gazette (*El Peruano*), on its website and through public hearings. Sunass provides plain language summaries and presentations of the studies on its website.

Stakeholders can submit comments at least 10 days before the public hearing and up to 5 business days afterwards, by letter or email, using forms provided on the regulator's website.

Once the draft tariff study is published and the date for the public hearing is set, a committee from the DRT, the DU and the relevant decentralised office communicate about the proposal, gather user's feedback and try to address any initial questions.

The public hearings are open to the EP, local authorities, professional associations, user councils, the media and civil society representatives, among others. They aim to provide information on challenges in the water and sanitation services, the proposed solutions and the impact on tariffs, and to gather comments from stakeholders. Sunass advertises its public hearings through several channels, including traditional media, its website, social media, newsletters, emails and on EP websites.

As with other economic regulators in Peru, Sunass prepares a <u>matrix that assembles stakeholders' comments</u>, and explains how the comments were taken into account or why they were not. This comments matrix is made public in the final Tariff Study.

The final Tariff Study is published on Sunass's website once approved by the Board, and the decision is also communicated through its decentralised offices.

Despite the public consultation processes, there remains frequent resistance to tariff increases. Rate-setting processes are sometimes disrupted by socio-political tensions. EPs do not always apply the rates that have been approved by Sunass. Furthermore, 19 out of the 50 EPs do not have up-to-date tariff studies.

Sunass has on occasion approved tariff studies that do not incorporate all required elements. For example, while regulations stipulate that EP's masterplans should give a 30-year vision, often they only cover a five-year horizon.

### Engagement in rural areas on the household fee

In rural areas, consumers pay a "household fee" (cuota familiar) that is set by the JASS. Sunass provides the methodology to calculate the household fee and has been training ATMs and JASS to implement the fee. The JASS changes every two years, which presents challenges for continuity of engagement. Rural providers appear to have low awareness and understanding of Sunass and its role.

According to Sunass regulations, the household fee must be set at a level that ensures the JASS can be self-sustaining. In general, the level of household fees set by JASS are insufficient to purchase necessary inputs (e.g. chlorine for water treatment), equipment or to employ an operator to maintain the infrastructure (as required by the regulations).

### Consultation on regulations

Draft regulations are also open to comment, although the regulator does not systematically hold public hearings to seek inputs from stakeholders. In the first instance, Sunass uses public consultation to identify the problem to be solved through the regulator's intervention. Sunass then invites comments from stakeholders on regulatory proposals. All comments along with Sunass's responses are published in the comments matrix that is available on the Sunass website.

### User Councils and spaces for citizen engagement

The Users Councils (*Consejo de Usuarios*, CU) are presented as a mechanism for the participation of civil society interested in improving the regulation of sanitation services, and are created for all Peruvian regulators following a legal requirement in the LMOR. Sunass has five Users Councils organised by regions. The North, South, East and Centre Users Councils are intended to be made up of five to six members, however, the review revealed that in practice these councils are made up of fewer members. Members are elected for two years: one member from each region chosen from among the candidates proposed by universities, professional associations, consumer associations and/or users recognised by Indecopi, business associations and non-profit civil associations. The Lima Users Council has five members, each of whom is chosen from among the candidates proposed by each type of the aforementioned organisations. Current members come largely from academia. There is also representation from chambers of commerce and NGOs. One of the councils includes a member from a consumer protection association.

The Lima Users Council meets monthly, whereas the other users' councils meet very rarely (once or twice during the two-year term). Although the council's functions include carrying out events on regulatory issues and transmitting users' queries about Sunass regulations or policies to the Board of Directors, in practice these activities are not carried out. The councils have no resources to enable them to engage with consumers or to review regulatory proposals.

Any proposals, consultations and contributions of the councils should be addressed to the Sunass Board of Directors. Opinions are non-binding. In practice, the councils very rarely submit opinions to Sunass. Any communications that are addressed to the regulator are made in writing, and are not published on the Sunass website.

Sunass also runs the "Participate, neighbour!" (*¡Participa, vecino!*) initiative, overseen by the Users Directorate. This offers a more informal platform for organised user groups (neighbourhood boards, building owner's board, merchant associations, etc.) to obtain information, dialogue, generate proposals and representation on different aspects related to the provision of sanitation services. In these spaces, citizens can find answers to their questions about their rights and duties, information on the sanitation service, complaints procedure, among other topics. In addition, they can have solutions agreed with their providers to problems that may arise, such as clogs and collapses of water or sewage, interrupted sanitation works and others. "Participate, neighbour!" is also intended to be a space for citizens to propose, through their Users Councils, some regulatory improvements to the regulator, although this does not appear to be taking place as the Users Councils are not interacting directly with consumers.

Under this initiative, using virtual platforms, Sunass organises talks and workshops to provide information; micro-hearings, in which representatives of the affected users and officials of the service provider are summoned to reach agreements to solve problems; and activities with members of the Users Councils to identify problems and present regulatory proposals. Micro-hearings are intended to be a mechanism to help users and providers reach agreement prior to or as an alternative to launching an official complaint, thereby saving time and increasing the social impact. The Users Directorate monitors if companies carry out actions they committed to during the micro-hearing. Utilities are not legally obliged to participate but in general agree to take part.

To participate, users are required to contact Sunass explaining the problem that affects them and their neighbours. A representative from Sunass then contacts them to schedule a virtual meeting with the main leaders of their area. Since the start of the Participate, Neighbour! Programme in June 2020 until June 2021, 343 micro-hearings were held and 996 talks and workshops on issues of user rights, regulation of providers and access to the service have been given. As of June 2021, over 18 000 people, mostly neighbourhood leaders, have participated in these spaces. The details of each meeting (micro-hearing, workshop or talk) are published monthly on the Sunass website.

### *Complaints*

Sunass provides users with complaint forms and guidelines on the procedure to follow on its website,[19] through a phone-line staffed by teams from its decentralised offices, and via social media.

Consumers must file complaints directly with their service provider. If their complaint is rejected twice by their service provider, they may appeal before Sunass's Claims Settlement Tribunal (TRASS). TRASS has up to 30 days in which to make its decision; on average decisions are taken within 15 days. To aid transparency, the process is digitised and complainants can track the progress of their file online.

TRASS decisions can be appealed in the judicial branch. Although the rate of appeal is very low (1%), this nevertheless represents a large number of cases (nearly 1 300 in 2020). The courts uphold TRASS decisions in over 90% of cases.

Sector insights gathered by TRASS are sometimes used to inform other areas of Sunass functions. For example, if TRASS identifies a large number of similar complaints, it will alert the Supervision and Enforcement directorates. In addition, TRASS carries out studies with consumers. One such study, requested by Board, highlighted a rise in the volume of complaints after price increases. As a result, Sunass developed guidance for providers about what to do following price increases.

In 2020, Peru's agency for consumer protection, Indecopi, proposed to create a "one-stop shop" for consumer complaints about public services, citing the complexity of the current system, and convened sector regulators including Sunass to take part in a technical working group to oversee the scheme.

### *Appeals*

Sunass decisions on regulations, sanctions and tariff determinations can be appealed. Sunass decisions may be challenged before the judiciary through a "contentious-administrative lawsuit" filed within three months of the notification of a decision. A judge in first instance makes a decision. This decision can be challenged, in which case the file is sent to the Superior Court, composed of three superior judges. Again, its decision can be appealed before the Supreme Court via "cassation appeal" (under certain grounds related to the non-application or incorrect application of the law), which decides through a collegiate composed of five supreme judges.

Likewise, the following constitutional processes can be initiated:

- Protective actions ("*Amparo*"): for the violation of some constitutional rights other than personal liberty. "Amparo" actions are initiated before a judge of the first instance; if the decision is challenged, the case is referred to a Superior Court and, against the latter's decision, an appeal is filed before the Constitutional Court, which is a constitutionally autonomous entity.
- Class Action ("*Acción Popular*"): directly against the regulatory provisions issued by Sunass and invoking violations of constitutional rights. Class Actions are initiated directly before a Superior Court, and an appeal of its decision causes the file to be referred to the Supreme Court. The Supreme Court's decision concludes the process.
- "Action of Unconstitutionality" proceedings: directly against a regulation of legal rank (Law, Legislative Decree) on which a Sunass prerogative is based, invoking violations of constitutional rights. "Action of Unconstitutionality" proceedings are only heard by the Constitutional Court, which issues a decision in a sole instance.

A relatively small number of Sunass decisions on regulations, sanctions or tariff determinations are appealed each year (Table 3.13), and Sunass reports it wins nearly all appeals. Most appeals are filed by regulated entities (rather than consumer groups, for example). In the case of sanctioning decisions, cases are filed against Sunass's General Management, as the Board does not take sanctioning decisions.

### Table 3.13. Appeals against Sunass decisions on regulations, sanctions and tariff determinations

| Year | Number of decisions taken | Number of decisions appealed | Status (decision upheld, rejected, ongoing) |
|------|---------------------------|------------------------------|---------------------------------------------|
| 2020 | 81 | 0 | - |
| 2019 | 59 | 3 | Ongoing |
| 2018 | 69 | 9 | 1 decision upheld 8 ongoing |
| 2017 | 113 | 9 | Ongoing |

Note: Decisions refer to regulations issued, sanctions/penalties imposed and tariff determinations.
Source: Information provided by Sunass, 2021.

TRASS decisions can also be appealed before the judicial branch (see section on Complaints, above). Ninety five per cent of the judicial proceedings against Sunass are appeals of TRASS resolutions.

## Output and outcome

### *Data collection, analysis and management*

Sunass has put in place two methods for data collection on service providers depending on location.

The 50 urban service providers (EPs) submit their data directly to Sunass using a system that has been in place since 2004. The data is used to calculate the tariffs established for the providers (using economic, financial, operational and quality data) and to monitor compliance with the management goals set for service providers (using data on continuity, pressure, number of new connections, wastewater treatment, etc.).

The data required is detailed in the General Supervision and Sanction Regulations[20] and the technical specifications of the required data is defined in a directive.[21] The Supervision Directorate periodically reviews the requirements for the provision of performance information and data. The last review occurred in 2019. However, the inclusion of new elements, discretionary changes or changes to definitions mean that the information collected is no longer aligned with the regulation in force.

In January 2019, Framework Law 1280 was modified to give technical units within municipalities (ATMs) the responsibility of reporting information to Sunass for supervision and oversight of community organisations. As of 2021, around 80% of ATMs report performance data to the ATM web system. Additionally, as part of its supervision activities, Sunass collects primary information from Communal Organisations in the field and places it in a database, as well as verifying the information from the ATM web system, if applicable. This information serves as the basis for the benchmarking of Communal Organisations and for supervising the quality of service. The regulator faces challenges in ensuring nationwide coverage of data collection, especially in remote and difficult to access areas of the country. So far Sunass has collected data from 2 000 of the 25 000 rural service providers through its ODS and local government ATMs.

A large volume of data is collected although the format in which it is published (e.g. PDFs) and the lack of inter-operability between systems constrains potential analysis and use. The process to validate and clean data is lengthy due to the lack of automation: it can take around six months from the time that data is collected to the moment that it is published as indicators.

Furthermore, the current IT infrastructure hinders data sharing and analysis within Sunass, with staff reporting that systems can't support multiple users working at the same time. The switch to remote working absorbed much of the capacity of the IT department in 2020, slowing progress on planned modernisation and improvement of IT systems. In addition, budget constraints limit the implementation of IT strategies, such as automation, digitalisation and the move to cloud-based systems.

Overall, data quality is poor due to inconsistency in data management practices and capacity constraints in service providers and other bodies (such as ATMs) that are required to submit data. In particular, there is a lack of reliable, standardised and timely data. Not all EPs gather the required information and those that do have different practices for managing, processing and saving data, making comparability a challenge. Furthermore, water utilities often miss deadlines for submitting information and data can be unreliable, despite being submitted as a sworn statement. For example, financial statements are not audited, but the data is compared with information sent by the EPs to the Public Accounting Office. As a result of inconsistencies in data and poor data quality, Sunass frequently has to go back to provider companies to make corrections to submitted data. Sunass also provides training to the water utility personnel responsible for processing and submitting the information; however, the high turnover of staff in water utilities means that this capacity is frequently lost and the regulator must regularly invest in training new personnel. Furthermore, it was reported during interviews that the public ownership of utilities results in politically appointed management positions.

Despite efforts, there is no integrated system of data collection and sharing between public institutions in the water and sanitation sector. Service providers and regional/local governments (e.g. ATMs) are often required to provide the same data to other public organisations in the sector. The MVCS leads the management and administration of the Water and Sanitation Information System (*Sistema de Información de Agua y Saneamiento*, SIAS), which is under construction at the time of writing, and its related Rural Water, Sanitation and Hygiene Information System (*Sistema de Diagnóstico sobre Abastecimiento de Agua y Saneamiento en el Ámbito Rural*, DATASS) platform covering rural areas, that is intended to integrate sanitation information. Separately, Sunass has developed the Data Capture and Transfer System (*Sistema de Captura y Transferencia de Datos*, SICAP) that collects information on management variables of the 50 EPs. The interoperability of the systems and databases is not yet effective across the board. A World Bank supported project aims to modernise and integrate datasystems on the sector across bodies, but progress to date has been slow.

The regulator's ability to obtain data and information from other public institutions in the sector tends to rely on personal relationships, rather than institutionalised agreements. Requests to other institutions are usually made via email between the technical teams.

### Monitoring and reporting on the performance of the sector

Sunass publishes a number of benchmarking reports:

- Annual Regulatory Benchmarking of Service Providers (https://www.sunass.gob.pe/productos-sunas/benchmarking-regulatorio/#1597358923084-6a5c292e-d2ab)
- Annual Benchmarking of Communal Organisations (https://www.sunass.gob.pe/productos-sunas/benchmarking-regulatorio/#1597510024732-47e43535-6f08)
- Quarterly Express Benchmarking of Service Providers (https://www.sunass.gob.pe/prestadores/empresas-prestadoras/indicadores-de-gestion/#1600223711840-09ce8705-08d4)
- Municipal Technical Area (ATM) Indicators Report (http://aplicaciones.sunass.gob.pe:8080/RegistroATM/indicadoresATM.html)

Sunass benchmarks EP performance in terms of access to services, quality of service, sustainability and governance (Table 3.14). Sunass is responsible for calculating indicators related to the service providers and contributes to the monitoring of compliance with the goals of the National Sanitation Plan through its indicators, as well as to the evaluation of compliance with the National Urban Sanitation Programme. Indicators related to the sector, such as drinking water and sewerage coverage at the national level, are calculated by the National Statistics Institute (*Instituto Nacional de Estadística e Informática*, INEI) through the National Survey of Budget Programs (*Encuesta Nacional de Programas Presupuestales*, ENAPRES) and are officially used by the MVCS.

### Table 3.14. Benchmarking indicators for service providers

| Type of indicator | Area | Indicator | Unit |
|---|---|---|---|
| Access | Drinking water | Population coverage | % |
| | Sewerage | Population coverage | % |
| Quality | Drinking water | Continuity of service | Hours/day |
| | | Water pressure | m.c.a. |
| | | Frequency of claims | No. claims/1000 connections |
| | | Prevalence of leakage | Leakage/km |
| | Sewerage | Clog density | clogs/km |
| Sustainability | Financial | Staff costs in total operating costs (*Working* | % |

| Type of indicator | Area | Indicator | Unit |
|---|---|---|---|
| | | relationship) | |
| | Prevention and mitigation | Disaster Risk Management | % |
| | Environmental | Non-domestic users within maximum permissible limits (*Non-Domestic Users in the application of Maximum Allowable Values* (VMA)) | % |
| | | Wastewater treated | % |
| | | Metered active connections (*Active Connections with Micrometering*) | % |
| | | Metered water (*Micrometering*) | % |
| | | Non-revenue water | % |
| Governance (*Gobernabilidad y Gobernanza*, GYG) | Good corporate governance | Indicator of good corporate governance | |

Source: Information provided by Sunass, 2021.

Sunass is in the process of updating the System of Indicators and Indices for the Management of Sanitation Services Providers (*Sistema de Indicadores e Índices de la Gestión de los Prestadores de los Servicios de Saneamiento*, SIIGEPSS) that will define performance indicators for the three different types of service providers: EPs, providers in small cities, and providers in rural areas.

The regulator's information portal presents various dashboards and databases covering different areas of work, including:

- performance indicators of rural providers;
- data on % of chlorinated water from MIDIS;
- data gathered by ATMs on rural providers;
- estimates of the reserve funds collected for the MERESE;
- data on guidance for consumers; awareness raising campaigns by the DSOs;
- georeferenced data showing location of service providers and Sunass ODS, number of households with access to services (GeoSunass); and
- data on coverage and continuity of service from the national statistics office.

However, many of the links are not working, although the regulator is working to resolve this problem. The data gathered by Sunass is published in several different formats, including in PDFs, xls, web pages and maps.

In 2021, Sunass launched a newsletter called "Sunass in Numbers" that presents key data on sector performance including rankings of service providers and data on sanctions and user enquiries.

Sunass is required to report on indicators other than the benchmarking of providers to several national organisations (e.g. INEI, MINAM, MVCS, PCM, INDECOPI, the Congress of the Republic, among others), as well as for international co-operation processes. Many of these are related to the Sustainable Development Goals, environmental indicators, and the volume of drinking water produced for the calculation of the national GDP.

Some data gathered by the regulator are not published due to their preliminary or confidential nature. Sunass only publishes processed data from the providers (i.e. indicators etc.), whereas the raw data collected is managed internally. Regarding data privacy, Sunass implements ISO 27001 on information security and adheres to Peru's national law for personal data protection.

### Monitoring and reporting on the performance of Sunass

At the highest level, Sunass's strategic plan includes eight indicators that span the regulator's five strategic objectives (Table 3.15). The indicators on "Percentage of users who value the importance of having sanitation services" and "Percentage of consumers who are willing to pay the set tariffs" have not been monitored as the sanitary situation due to the Covid-19 pandemic meant that Sunass was unable to carry out the necessary user perception surveys.

### Table 3.15. Sunass performance indicators

| Code. | OEI | Indicator | Goals | | | | |
|---|---|---|---|---|---|---|---|
| | | | 2020 | 2021 | 2022 | 2023 | 2024 |
| OEI.01 | Strengthen the provision of sanitation services to the user. | Index of the Management and Provision of Sanitation Services of the Provider Companies (IGPSS). | 76.31% | 78.86% | 81.41% | 83.96% | 84.01% |
| | | Percentage of providers in rural areas with good management. | 25.05% | 25.88% | 26.72% | 27.56% | 28.41% |
| OEI.02 | Consolidate the decentralisation of Sunass functions. | Percentage of ODSs showing optimal performance in the performance of de-concentrated functions. | 70% | 80% | 90% | 100% | 100% |
| OEI.03 | Improve the perception and appreciation of sanitation services by users. | Percentage of users who value the importance of having sanitation services. | 3% | 5% | 10% | 15% | 10% |
| | | Percentage of users satisfied with Sunass services | 50% | 55% | 60% | 70% | 75% |
| | | Percentage of users of sanitation services who are willing to pay the set tariffs. | 0% | 5% | 10% | 15% | 20% |
| OEI.04 | Strengthening Institutional Management | Percentage of internal clients satisfied with the services provided by line bodies. | 60% | 65% | 70% | 75% | 80% |
| OEI.05 | Implement disaster risk management | Percentage of implementation of Disaster Risk Management Plan. | 50% | 60% | 70% | 80% | 90% |

Source: Information provided by Sunass, 2021.

Sunass links up the data on its strategic goals with financial information to monitor the cost per indicator. Monitoring is done by line management and the OPPM.

The regulator also monitors a range of indicators of organisational performance that capture aspects of efficiency, effectiveness, the quality of regulatory processes, and the direct outcomes of decisions (e.g. compliance with decisions), for example:

- Number of tariff studies approved in the year
- Cost per tariff study
- Proportion of tariff studies that are up-to-date
- The number of providers with tariff studies in force
- The number of supervision and monitoring reports concluded during the year
- The number of providers that comply with submitting periodic information
- Index of compliance with management goals established in the tariff studies.

While Sunass is not required to so do so by law, it prepares an annual report. The last annual report was produced in 2019. The regulator also reports on its performance to a number of central government entities. For instance, it reports on the implementation of recommendations to the CGR, budget execution to the MEF; and strategic and operational plans and performance indicators to the PCM, among others.

There is no obligation to provide performance reports to Congress on a systematic basis. However, every year Sunass reports on its management, achievements and challenges to two congressional commissions: Housing and Construction; and Consumer Protection and Regulatory Agencies of Public Utilities. It also responds to information requests and enquiries from Congress on a regular basis. For example, these Commissions have summoned Sunass to make presentations on specific issues such as tariff updates or problems in the sector.

## Notes

[1] https://www.sunass.gob.pe/sunass/quienes-somos/.

[2] MERESE – akin to the concept of Payments for Ecosystem Services (*Pagos por Servicios Ecosistémicos*, PSE) – aims to mobilise funds from downstream users, through a percentage of the water tariff, to upstream providers for the conservation of water resources and the basins where they come from. Source: https://iwa-network.org/mechanisms-of-rewards-for-ecosystem-services-mrse/.

[3] https://busquedas.elperuano.pe/normaslegales/decreto-legislativo-que-regula-el-regimen-especial-de-monito-decreto-legislativo-n-1185-1275103-1/.

[4] As established in paragraph 97.2 of article 97 of the Single Ordered Text of the Administrative Procedure Law (approved by Supreme Decree No. 004-2019-JUS). According to Article 42(g) of the Rules of Organization and Powers of the Presidency of the Council of Ministers, approved by Supreme Decree No. 022-2017-PCM, the Secretariat of Public Management is responsible for issuing technical opinions on any conflict of functions.

[5] Approved by Supreme Decree No. 004-2019-JUS.

[6] The Regulatory Quality Analysis (Análisis de Calidad Regulatoria) is a tool introduced by the PCM for use by agencies to identify the administrative burden of new regulation (i.e. formalities or procedures required). Regulation: http://www.pcm.gob.pe/wp-content/uploads/2017/08/Decreto_Supremo_075-2017-PCM.pdf; Technical guidelines: http://www.pcm.gob.pe/wp-content/uploads/2017/08/ManualAC.pdf.

[7] The contribution rate from industry is approved by the Executive through a Supreme Decree endorsed by the President of the Council of Ministers and MEF. Promotion taxes refer to the Municipal Promotion Tax as mentioned in Law No. 27332.

[8] The support and advisory offices include OAF, OPPM, OAJ, OTI and OCII.

[9] At the end of 2020, 10.5% of the total budget used for personnel payments at the national level was spent on external contractors/consultants.

[10] Published in El Peruano, 3 October 2020.

[11] Service Provision Area Directorate, Policies and Norms Directorate, and the Sanctions Directorate.

[12] Information as of 12 March 2021.

[13] El Peruano, 2 October 2020: Approval of the Cadre for the Assignment of Provisional Personnel – CAP Provisional of the National Superintendence of Sanitation Services (Sunass), Ministerial Resolution No. 277-2020-PCM, Lima.

[14] E.g. The opinions on the Sanitation Services Concession Contract of the South Lima districts or on the Puerto Maldonado Wastewater Treatment Plant Concession Contract are not published.

[15] To date, the only contract that falls under the PPP modality where Sunass has supervisory responsibilities is the concession contract for the Wastewater Treatment System of the Lake Titicaca Basin project. The contract stipulates the matters that are subject to supervision by Sunass and include contractual, legal, technical and administrative obligations in accordance with applicable laws and provisions, including the supervision of service levels.

[16] In line with regulations DS 096-2007-PC, which regulates subsequent random auditing of administrative procedures by the State, and Board of Directors Resolution 014-2008-SUNASS-CD Directive on Subsequent Auditing of Administrative Procedures of SUNASS.

[17] According to the Regulation of Water Quality for Human Consumption.

[18] Based on the sampling frequency approved in Board of Directors Resolution No. 015-2012-SUNASS-CD.

[19] Other request forms (for example, for problems not related to billing or operational issues, or requests to change a water meter, among others) are also available to download free of charge through the same website.

[20] Under Annex 2, "Transfer of Periodic Information from the EP to SUNASS".

[21] Circular notice No. 178-2019/SUNASS/030, http://nube.sunass.gob.pe/index.php/s/22cqu7dusxi4eyt.

## References

OECD (2021), *Water Governance in Peru*, OECD Studies on Water, OECD Publishing, Paris, https://dx.doi.org/10.1787/568847b5-en. [2]

OECD (2020), *Regulatory Enforcement and Inspections in the Environmental Sector of Peru*, OECD Publishing, Paris, https://dx.doi.org/10.1787/54253639-en. [3]

OECD (2015), *The Governance of Water Regulators*, OECD Studies on Water, OECD Publishing, Paris, https://dx.doi.org/10.1787/9789264231092-en. [1]

# Annex A. Methodology

Measuring regulatory performance is challenging, starting with defining what to measure, dealing with confounding factors, attributing outcomes to interventions and coping with the lack of data and information. This annex describes the methodology developed by the OECD to help regulators address these challenges through a Performance Assessment Framework for Economic Regulators (PAFER), which informs this review. It first presents some of the work conducted by the OECD on measuring regulatory performance. It then describes the key features of the PAFER and presents a typology of performance indicators to measure input, process, output and outcome. It finally provides an overview of the approach and practical steps undertaken for developing this review.

This Annex summarises the methodology developed by the OECD to assess regulatory authorities' governance arrangements, drivers of performance as well as their performance measurement matrices. The methodology was prepared based on the experience of regulators participating in the OECD Network of Economic Regulators and the present report constitutes its thirteenth application to a regulatory body. Other reviews spanning a number of sectors and countries include: Colombia's Communications Regulation Commission (OECD, 2015[1]); Latvia's Public Utilities Commission (OECD, 2016[2]), Mexico's three energy regulators (OECD, 2017[3]), (OECD, 2017[4]), (OECD, 2017[5]), (OECD, 2017[6]); Ireland's Commission for Regulation of Utilities (OECD, 2018[7]); Peru's Energy and Mining Regulator (OECD, 2019[8]); Peru's Telecommunications Regulator (OECD, 2019[9]), Peru's Transport Infrastructure Regulator (OECD, 2020[10]) Ireland's Environmental Protection Agency (OECD, 2020[11]), Portugal's Energy Services Regulatory Authority (OECD, 2021[12]) and Brazil's Electricity Regulatory Authority (OECD, 2021[13]). The methodology has been adapted since its first application to learnings throughout the review process and is adjusted to take into account specific needs and contextual characteristics of each regulator, sector and jurisdiction.

## Analytical framework

The analytical framework that informs this review draws on OECD work on measuring regulatory performance and the governance of economic regulators. OECD countries and regulators have recognised the need for measuring regulatory performance. Information on regulatory performance is necessary to better target scarce resources and to improve the overall performance of regulatory policies and regulators. However, measuring regulatory performance can prove challenging. Some of these challenges include:

- *What to measure*: evaluation systems require an assessment of how inputs have influenced outputs and outcomes. In the case of regulatory policy, the inputs can focus on: i) overall programmes intended to promote a systemic improvement of regulatory quality; ii) the application of specific practices intended to improve regulation, or iii) changes in the design of specific regulations.

- *Confounding factors*: there is a myriad of contingent issues that have an impact on the outcomes in society which regulation is intended to affect. These issues can be as simple as a change in the weather, or as complicated as the last financial crisis. Accordingly, it is difficult to establish a direct causal relationship between the adoption of better regulation practices and specific improvements to the welfare outcomes that are sought in the economy.

- *Lack of data and information*: countries tend to lack data and methodologies to identify whether regulatory practices are being undertaken correctly and what impact these practices may be having on the real economy.

The OECD (2014[14]) *Framework for Regulatory Policy Evaluation* starts addressing these challenges through an input-process-output-outcome logic, which breaks down the regulatory process into a sequence of discrete steps. The input-process-output-outcome logic is flexible and can be applied both to evaluate practices to improve regulatory policy in general, and also to evaluate regulatory policy in specific sectors, based on the identification of relevant strategic objectives. It can be tailored to economic regulators by taking into consideration the conditions that support the performance of economic regulators (Box A A.1).

The OECD Best Practice Principles for Regulatory Policy: The Governance of Regulators (OECD, 2014[15]) identifies some of the conditions that support the performance of economic regulators. They recognise the importance of assessing how a regulator is directed, controlled, resourced and held to account, in order to improve the overall effectiveness of regulators and promote growth and investment, including by supporting competition. Moreover, they acknowledge the positive impact of the regulator's own internal process on outcomes (i.e. how the regulator manages resources and what processes the regulator puts in place to regulate a given sector or market) (Figure A A.1).

**Box A A.1. The input-process-output-outcome logic sequence**

- **Step I. Input**: indicators include, for example, the budget and staff of the regulatory oversight body.

- **Step II. Process**: indicators assess whether formal requirements for good regulatory practices are in place. This includes requirements for objective setting, consultation, evidence-based analysis, administrative simplification, risk assessments and aligning regulatory changes internationally.

- **Step III. Output**: indicators provide information on whether the good regulatory practices have actually been implemented.

- **Step IV. Impact of design on outcome (also referred to as intermediate outcome):** indicators assess whether good regulatory practices contributed to an improvement in the quality of regulations. It therefore attempts to make a causal link between the design of regulatory policy and outcomes.

- **Step V. Strategic outcomes**: indicators assess whether the desired outcomes of regulatory policy have been achieved, both in terms of regulatory quality and in terms of regulatory outcomes.

Source: (OECD, 2014[14]).

**Figure A A.1. The OECD Best Practice Principles on the Governance of Regulators**

Source: Adapted from (OECD, 2014[15]).

The two frameworks are brought together into a Performance Assessment Framework for Economic Regulators that structures the drivers of performance along the input-process-output-outcome framework (Table A A.1).

## Table A A.1. Criteria for assessing regulators' own performance framework

| References | Strategic objectives | Input | Process | Output and outcome |
|---|---|---|---|---|
| Best Practice Principles for the Governance of Regulators | • Role clarity | • Funding | • Maintaining trust and preventing undue influence | • Performance evaluation |
| | | | • Decision making and governing body structure | |
| | | | • Accountability and transparency | |
| | | | • Engagement | |
| Institutional, organisational and monitoring drivers | • Objectives and targets | • Budgeting and financial management | • Strategy, leadership and co-ordination | • Performance standards and indicators |
| | • Functions and powers | • Human resources management | • Institutional structure | • Performance processes and reports |
| | | | • Management systems and operating processes | • Feedback or outside evidence on performance |
| | | | • Relations and interfaces with Government bodies, regulated entities and other key stakeholders | |
| | | | • Regulatory management tools | |

Source: OECD Analysis.

## Performance indicators

For regulators, performance indicators need to fit the purpose of performance assessment, which is a systematic, analytical evaluation of the regulator's activities, with the purpose of seeking reliability and usability of the regulator's activities. Performance assessment is neither an audit, which judges how employees and managers complete their mission, nor a control, which puts emphasis on compliance with standards (OECD, 2004[16]).

Accordingly, performance indicators need to assess the efficient and effective use of a regulator's inputs, the quality of regulatory processes, and identify outputs and some direct outcomes that can be attributed to the regulator's interventions. Wider outcomes should serve as a "watchtower", which provides the information the regulator can use to identify problem areas, orient decisions and identify priorities (Figure A A.2).

### Figure A A.2. Input-process-output-outcome framework for performance indicators

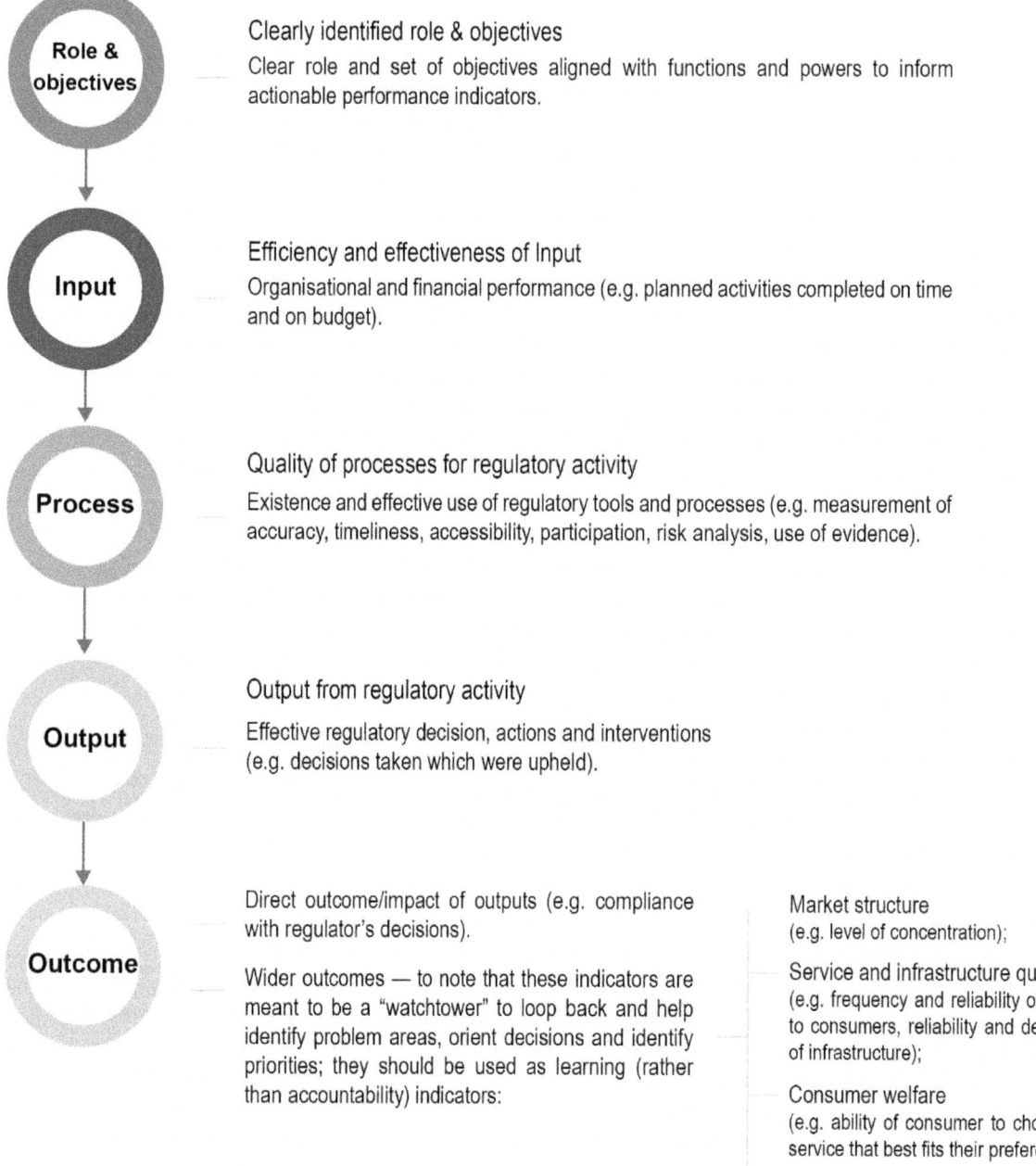

**Clearly identified role & objectives**
Clear role and set of objectives aligned with functions and powers to inform actionable performance indicators.

**Efficiency and effectiveness of Input**
Organisational and financial performance (e.g. planned activities completed on time and on budget).

**Quality of processes for regulatory activity**
Existence and effective use of regulatory tools and processes (e.g. measurement of accuracy, timeliness, accessibility, participation, risk analysis, use of evidence).

**Output from regulatory activity**
Effective regulatory decision, actions and interventions (e.g. decisions taken which were upheld).

Direct outcome/impact of outputs (e.g. compliance with regulator's decisions).

Wider outcomes — to note that these indicators are meant to be a "watchtower" to loop back and help identify problem areas, orient decisions and identify priorities; they should be used as learning (rather than accountability) indicators:

Market structure
(e.g. level of concentration);

Service and infrastructure quality
(e.g. frequency and reliability of services to consumers, reliability and deployment of infrastructure);

Consumer welfare
(e.g. ability of consumer to choose the service that best fits their preferences);

Industry performance
(e.g. revenues, profitability, investment).

Notes: This framework was proposed in the initial methodology for the performance assessment framework for economic regulators (PAFER) discussed with the OECD Network of Economic Regulators (NER). It has been refined to reflect feedback from NER members and the experience of other regulators in assessing their own performance.
Source: (OECD, 2015[1]), Figure 3.3 (updated in 2017).

## Approach

The analytical framework presented above informed the data collection and the analysis presented in the report. The present report looks at the internal and external governance arrangements of Peru's Water and Sanitation Services Regulator (Sunass) in the following areas:

- **Role and objectives**: to identify the existence of a set of clearly identified objectives, targets, or goals that are aligned with the regulator's functions and powers, which can inform the development of actionable performance indicators;
- **Input**: to determine the extent to which the regulator's funding and staffing are aligned with the regulator's objectives, targets or goals, and the regulator's ability to manage financial and human resources autonomously and effectively;
- **Process**: to assess the extent to which processes and the organisational management support the regulator's performance;
- **Output and outcome**: to identify the existence of a systematic assessment of the performance of the regulated entities, the impact of the regulator's decisions and activities, and the extent to which these measurements are used appropriately.

Data informing the analysis presented in the report was collected via a desk review, two fact-finding missions and a peer mission:

- **Questionnaire and desk review:** Sunass completed a detailed questionnaire which informed a desk review by the OECD Secretariat. The Secretariat reviewed existing legislation and Sunass documents to collect information on the *de jure* functioning of the regulator, and to inform the fact-finding missions. This questionnaire was tailored to Sunass, based on the methodology already applied by the OECD to other regulators since 2015 and on the participation of Sunass in former OECD research such as the 2021 *Water Governance in Peru* publication.

- **Fact-finding missions:** the first fact-finding mission focused on meeting Sunass internal teams and was conducted by the OECD Secretariat between 3 June – 11 June 2021. The second fact-finding mission took place between 21 June – 25 June 2021 and focused primarily on meeting external stakeholders. These missions were the key tool to collect and complete the *de jure* information obtained through the questionnaire with the *de facto* state of play. The work of the fact-finding missions tailored the PAFER methodology to Sunass's features. Information collected was completed and checked with Sunass for accuracy. Both missions were virtual due to the context of the COVID-19 pandemic.

- **Peer mission:** the peer mission took place between 6 September – 10 September 2021 and included peer reviewers from Italy, Portugal and the United States, in addition to the OECD Secretariat. This mission met with key stakeholders in Sunass as well as externally. At the end of the mission, the team discussed preliminary findings and recommendations with senior management from Sunass to test their feasibility. This mission was conducted remotely via videoconference.

During the fact-finding and peer missions, the team met with Sunass leadership team as well as a number of staff from across the institution. In addition, the team met with government institutions and external stakeholders, including:

- Presidency of the Council of Ministers (PCM)
- Ministry of Housing, Construction and Sanitation (MVCS)
- General Directorate of Environmental Affairs (DGAA)
- Ministry of Environment (MINAM)
- Ministry of Development and Social Inclusion (MIDIS)

- National Water Authority (ANA)
- Technical Organisation for the Administration of Sanitation Services (OTASS)
- Private Investment Promotion Agency (ProInversion)
- National Institute for the Defense of Competition and the Protection of Intellectual Property (INDECOPI)
- Municipal Technical Authorities (ATMs) of Cusco and Los Baños del Inca
- Regional Goverment of Housing, Construction and Sanitation of Arequipa, Ayacucho and Tumbes
- Congressional Commission of Housing, Construction and Sanitation
- Sedapal
- EMAPA Chancay
- National Association of Sanitation Service Providers of Peru (ANEPSSA)
- Rural Sanitation Services Administrative Boards (JASS) of Namora, San José and Santo Tomás
- Representatives of Users Councils (East, Lima and South)
- World Bank

## References

OECD (2021), *Driving Performance at Brazil's Electricity Regulatory Agency*, The Governance of Regulators, OECD Publishing, Paris, https://dx.doi.org/10.1787/11824ef6-en. [13]

OECD (2021), *Driving Performance at Portugal's Energy Services Regulatory Authority*, The Governance of Regulators, OECD Publishing, Paris, https://dx.doi.org/10.1787/05fb2fae-en. [12]

OECD (2020), *Driving Performance at Ireland's Environmental Protection Agency*, The Governance of Regulators, OECD Publishing, Paris, https://dx.doi.org/10.1787/009a0785-en. [11]

OECD (2020), *Driving Performance at Peru's Transport Infrastructure Regulator*, The Governance of Regulators, OECD Publishing, Paris, https://dx.doi.org/10.1787/d4ddab52-en. [10]

OECD (2019), *Driving Performance at Peru's Energy and Mining Regulator*, The Governance of Regulators, OECD Publishing, Paris, https://dx.doi.org/10.1787/9789264310865-en. [8]

OECD (2019), *Driving Performance at Peru's Telecommunications Regulator*, The Governance of Regulators, OECD Publishing, Paris, https://dx.doi.org/10.1787/9789264310506-en. [9]

OECD (2018), *Driving Performance at Ireland's Commission for Regulation of Utilities*, The Governance of Regulators, OECD Publishing, Paris, http://dx.doi.org/10.1787/9789264190061-en. [7]

OECD (2017), *Driving Performance at Mexico's Agency for Safety, Energy and Environment*, The Governance of Regulators, OECD Publishing, Paris, https://dx.doi.org/10.1787/9789264280458-en. [6]

OECD (2017), *Driving Performance at Mexico's Energy Regulatory Commission*, The Governance of Regulators, OECD Publishing, Paris, https://dx.doi.org/10.1787/9789264280830-en. [4]

OECD (2017), *Driving Performance at Mexico's National Hydrocarbons Commission*, The Governance of Regulators, OECD Publishing, Paris, https://dx.doi.org/10.1787/9789264280748-en. [5]

OECD (2017), *Driving Performance of Mexico's Energy Regulators*, The Governance of Regulators, OECD Publishing, Paris, https://dx.doi.org/10.1787/9789264267848-en. [3]

OECD (2016), *Driving Performance at Latvia's Public Utilities Commission*, The Governance of Regulators, OECD Publishing, Paris, https://dx.doi.org/10.1787/9789264257962-en. [2]

OECD (2015), *Driving Performance at Colombia's Communications Regulator*, OECD Publishing, Paris, https://dx.doi.org/10.1787/9789264232945-en. [1]

OECD (2014), *OECD Framework for Regulatory Policy Evaluation*, OECD Publishing, Paris, https://dx.doi.org/10.1787/9789264214453-en. [14]

OECD (2014), *The Governance of Regulators*, OECD Best Practice Principles for Regulatory Policy, OECD Publishing, Paris, https://dx.doi.org/10.1787/9789264209015-en. [15]

OECD (2004), *The choice of tools for enhancing policy impact: Evaluation and review*, OECD, Paris, http://www.oecd.org/officialdocuments/publicdisplaydocumentpdf/?cote=gov/pgc(2004)4&docl anguage=en (accessed on 16 November 2018). [16]